To Norma Jeane With Love, Jimmie,

by

Jim Dougherty

as told to LC Van Savage

BeachHouse Books

Chesterfield, Missouri

Copyright

Graphics Credits:

Front cover: taken by photographer Joseph Jasgur (now in Orlando, Florida). This was the photo Norma Jeane told Joe she wanted taken, to save and give to "my Jimmie" when he came home from serving in the Merchant Marine in World War II. she told Joe that day how much she loved Jimmie. The Picture of Jim and Rita Dougherty is courtesy of the Portland Magazine, website www.portlandmonthly.com

Aside from photographs provided by Joseph Jasgur and Portland Magazine, other photographs are from the private collection of the author, Jim Dougherty.

First BeachHouse Books Edition ISBN 1-888725-51-6 January, 2001
MacroPrint Books Edition ISBN 1-888725-52-4, January, 2001

Library of Congress Cataloging-in-Publication Data
Dougherty, Jim, 1921-
  To Norma Jeane with love, Jimmie / by Jim Dougherty as told to LC Van Savage.
       p. cm.
   ISBN 1-888725-51-6

Published: Chesterfield, Mo. : BeachHouse Books, 2001.
1. Monroe, Marilyn, 1926-1962 -- Relations with men. 2. Dougherty, Jim, 1921- -- Relations with women. 3. Motion picture actors and actresses -- United States -- Biography. I. Van Savage, LC, 1938- II. Title.
   PN2287.M67 D64 2001
   791.43'028'092--dc21

                                        00-012855

BeachHouse Books

www.beachhousebooks.com

an Imprint of
Science & Humanities Press
PO Box 7151
Chesterfield, MO 63006-7151
(636) 394-4950
www.beachhousebooks.com

Dedication:

This book is for Rita Dougherty, my beloved wife who lives with me, loves me, makes me laugh and lets me win at cribbage. Rita has come to love Norma Jeane as I do, and she has given me her love, support and endless encouragement. I cannot imagine life without my beautiful Rita.

Acknowledgments:

I will never be able to give enough thanks to photographer Joe Jasgur and his wife Debbie, two remarkable and kind people, enough for their incredible generosity in giving me this book's beautiful photographs of Norma Jeane, most of which were taken by Joe, and all taken while Norma Jeane and I were married. The front cover photo is the photo Norma Jeane told Joe she wanted taken, to save and give to "my Jimmie" when he came home from serving in the Merchant Marine in World War II. she told Joe that day how much she loved me.

I will always remember Eleanor (Beebe) Goddard, Norma Jeane's foster sister. She was important to all of us.

Paul Kanteman is my nephew and was Norma Jeane's and my ringbearer at our wedding. I wish to mention him here because he and I are still close and, as an eleven year old, he was Norma Jeane's constant companion while I was overseas.

Jack Clemmons; I won't ever forget that he was the man who called me first to tell me about Norma Jeane's death so I would not have to hear it on the news, thereby giving me a chance to escape before the reporters swarmed.

I will always love the Los Angeles Police Department for giving me a wonderful, fulfilling career, allowing me to do something with my life that I loved. and I will never forget them for protecting me when Norma Jeane died.

And lastly, I wish to give a tip of my hat to all the Marilyn Monroe fan clubs everywhere for their kindness and support of me over the years. they are one very fine group of people and I am honored to be a part of them.

LC and I want to thank publisher Bud Banis and publicist Tommy Garrett for their invaluable and selfless work in making our book a success.

J.D.

To Norma Jeane With Love, Jimmie,

by

Jim Dougherty

CHAPTER 1

It's been more than three decades since the phone rang in my home before dawn that Sunday. I'd been used to phones ringing at all hours because of my years of working on the Los Angeles Police Department, but there was something about this particular ring. I sat up, completely awake, as if I'd been up for hours. I turned and looked at the phone and some part of me, deep within, pressed down and flat. A drenching chill flashed through me and I shuddered. I watched my hand as if it were not mine as it reached for the receiver. It was cold and hard against my ear. I knew I did not want to hear the words that would come through it, the words I'd always known were one day coming.

I recognized the voice. It was my good friend from the Los Angeles Police Department, Sergeant Jack Clemens, and I did not hear him when he told me they'd found her dead in bed. I did not hear those terrible words coming from my old friend going straight into my ears and my heart, and yet there they were, expected, dreaded, and his voice was clear and I knew. I knew Jack was finally saying them because I'd always known someone would say them to me someday. I can't say why I knew, but I did. I thought the hearing of them would be easier, rehearsed over the years in my mind as they had been. And yet when Jack finished speaking, a smashing numbness collapsed me inside, outside, my eyes, my hearing, my belly, and I could not breathe, or see or hear.

Suicide they told me later. But no. She would never have done that. Not her. I turned and looked down at my wife Pat. She stared up at me from the pillow, her eyes wide, questioning.

"Say a prayer, " I said, my voice breaking. "Norma Jeane is dead."

To the world, she was and always will be Marilyn Monroe, but to me, she was Norma Jeane Baker who happily became Norma Jeane Dougherty, taking my name because she so desperately wanted to be part of a family, to belong to someone forever, someone who would love her always and would not leave her. I promised her I never would, and I kept that promise.

It's been over five decades since Norma Jeane and I were together. The years haven't in the least diminished my memories of that glowing, sweet child-woman I still love so dearly. I am not ashamed to say here or to the world that my eyes fill when I speak of her and our too-short time together. I see Norma Jeane nearly every day, and not just in my dreams and thoughts. She is everywhere I look; on posters, sweatshirts, T-shirts, mugs, life-sized cutouts propped in doorways, calendars. She is in every store I go into, seen every day on television, in every library, in thousands of books, tapes, and movies. I hear her recorded voice, so different from the high pitched sweet little child voice she had when we were married, but they made her lower it. Ah, but after all, she was only a little girl when we married. Norma Jeane was just two weeks into her 16th year in 1941 when we exchanged our vows and promised to love each other until our deaths.

And so Norma Jeane's gone, but she left long before she died. In a very short period of time, just a couple of years, Norma Jeane Dougherty, born a Gemini (the Twins) willingly became absorbed and taken over by the Marilyn Monroe twin. It wasn't a "good twin bad twin" theory, and really I don't pay that much attention to all that star and planet stuff, but there were two people within my beloved Norma Jeane and the Marilyn part of her was the stronger and more convincing. Settling down with me, a man who would probably not make a lot of money and who wanted a bunch of kids and a happy simple life, couldn't really compete with what she perceived as a wildly glamorous life with lots of money, cars, homes, and of course, the adulation of the world. But I have never for one single day forgotten the Norma Jeane part of Marilyn Monroe and I know absolutely it's true that the world has never forgotten the Marilyn part of Norma Jeane.

I'm older now and as my life winds down, I find myself yearning to tell Norma Jeane about all the joy she gave to me. And it wasn't as if I hadn't realized it was happening all the while it was happening; I knew. I knew I'd been given something unique in my life, I was well aware that other men had wives they adored, but something always told me my wife was different, that she'd "stepped out of the line" as they say, that she had a certain aura or quality — it's hard to define even today---and I always told her these things that back then. I remember.

But today I wonder; did I tell her often enough? Did I let her know she was my very world? That I adored her heart, respected her mind and worshipped her beauty? I wonder if she believed me back then. She'd smile and thank me, sometimes her beautiful eyes filling with tears when she listened to me say those things, but was she able to believe me? Were my words of love I said to her just too late? Had the poison already seeped into her mind? Had she been abandoned so often that she could no longer see herself as beautiful? Had she been abandoned so often that she finally came to believe it must be her fault, that she was so ugly and so bad no one could possibly want her?

I've had so much time to think about those things; time that came after the hurt had healed and I'd gotten on with my successful and very happy life. As the years passed, I've found myself wanting to ask her "why, Norma Jeane? Why did you leave me? We were so happy. We loved each other so dearly. You told me that so often. We told each other."

But of course I know why . I know that the promise of great fame, vast amounts of money, of no more worries, the glamour, the company of famous, glittering people, and above all else, the adulation of millions ---all of these were the reasons you left me. I could provide you none of them. All I had to give was a good, simple life, filled with kindness, love, children and happiness. All of these simple pleasures must have suddenly seemed terribly dull to you when you saw that big, shiny Hollywood finger crook at you and beckon you to come.

I'm getting older now and find I'm now often wishing I could speak again with my Norma Jeane, wishing I could tell her these things, to thank her even now, so long after her death, although it was the death which ultimately robbed me of the chance to thank her. But then, when I think with my head and not my heart, I know I'd never have gotten the chance to tell her this. She wouldn't have been able to hear me anyway, once she became "her."

I was a stranger to Marilyn Monroe. If she ever spoke of me, it was quickly. She would say she wished me happiness. That our marriage had been one of convenience. And so in time, she never spoke of me again. Marilyn Monroe did not know me although the Norma Jeane that buried so deeply within her always did. But Marilyn was someone else, a being separate from Norma Jeane, the young girl who added rainbows and laughter to my life, my whole life, during our time together certainly, but long afterward too, right until this day. I can't forget. I never want to.

Los Angeles, April 12, 1921. I was born an Aries, sign of the ram. I like that. And at times in my life I am proud to say I was that-- strong, rugged, wilderness loving, free, confrontational, and often quite vigorously in rut.

1937. This was my year. I was sixteen, my hormones were singing loudly to me and I was paying very close attention. I owned a 1927 Buick, had enough money from my summer job to make good use of that car, and "good use" to young men back then (and still today) meant only one thing; dates. Girls. That's all there was and all I needed. Dates and girls were the only reasons I, or any young man, lived, then or now. Life was looking very sweet to me in 1937. I was a senior in highschool, on the football team, acting and singing whenever I could, president of the student council, but oh, how I loved the girls. It was time for Jim Dougherty to howl and nothin' was gonna hold me back!

Well, at least nothing that didn't involve money! There wasn't much of it, after all. My family was poor. But then, everybody's was back then, so that's a statement of fact and not a plea for pity. Both of my parents, my two older brothers Tom and Marion, and my sister Billie. all worked to keep the family fed, clothed and sheltered. It's how it was done during that difficult time in our country's history, during the Great Depression. (Old joke, but I've got to ask--- "what was great about it?") No one complained about his or her poorness. It was all we kids knew, after all, and we were content. We loved our lives.

I became a crack shot at a very young age. Bullets, when I was a child, were expensive and since it often fell to me to bring dinner home from the California hills, that animal or bird had to go down deader than hell with one shot and one shot only. There was not enough money for a two-bullet dinner! And even though we could not afford to waste ammunition, we were also taught that an animal must not be allowed to suffer, that when we shot, it was to be a quick and perfect kill. I learned. The ability to shoot once, straight, and accurately would serve me well all my life and especially during my years on the Los Angeles Police Department.

My father finally got a job that paid a little more than the one he had previously, and we moved back to California from Globe, Arizona, when I was six or seven. When the Great Depression hit, we found ourselves living in a very old car and a tent, not a terribly unusual occurrence for that time.

But finally, in the fall of 1930, the entire family had actually saved enough money from picking apricots in an orchard, to rent a tiny house in Van Nuys, so tiny that two of us had to go back and live in that tent again out in the front yard. But we always ate. We always had clothes (patched and old, but clothes nonetheless) and we were a family, solid, unbreakable, and together. "Family" meant something strong and all-important to everyone back then and especially to all of us, and that sense of unified strength has stayed with me. Family, marriage and children; these are the basic reasons I exist today. And they were the fundamental reasons Norma Jeane could not stay with me.

I expect readers of my story will wonder about this, having read as so many have that Marilyn Monroe yearned so for children, so desperately desired a home and family. And this has confused me over the years too, because as you will read later, when we were newly married, she wanted children so badly, loved being a homemaker, and spoke so often about the happiness she'd found with me, living in her first real home, and planning for future babies.

But Hollywood is a seductive entity, offering temptations beyond the wildest dreams of the young actors and actresses yearning to go "out there" and "get in the movies." It dangles money and excitement, travel and glamour in front of young eager eyes. But, when they beckoned to her, the Hollywood people told Norma Jeane she couldn't be married, because back then young ladies only became pregnant when married, (or at least were supposed to, but didn't always, just like today) and of course, as a young starlet, she could not be pregnant. Married women, and worse, married pregnant women, or worse, married women with children were considered no longer sexy or glamorous. They were used up, sexless has-beens, worthless and worth nothing financially, and the studios invested too much money in their starlets to allow them to get into those sorts of "situations."

CHAPTER 2

But back to those glory years for me, the 1930's. I will confess to being a ham when I was young, a weakness or maybe even a passion I still experience today, in my late seventies. I just simply love to perform and have absolutely no fear of it. Stagefright? What's that?? By the time I was twelve, I was a fiddle player for local dances and learned the harmonica and guitar too. I loved to sing and would perform whenever requested, (and frequently when not.) I was a leading man in the Maskers, a high school drama group and another hammy type played my daughter in a play called *Shirtsleeves*, at Van Nuys High School. Her name was Jane Russell and we've remained lifetime friends and still keep in touch. I took first place in my class at Occidental College in a Shakespearean Festival Contest when I recited Shylock's "revenge" speech. I know that had the opportunity presented itself, I would have pursued a career in acting, but life often gets in the way of our dreams, and it was not to be. (Not until recently, that is.)

And I will also confess immodestly to being a jock in those days, loving sports and playing football, and also getting involved in politics on a secondary level. I enjoyed being student body president. I loved the limelight, loved being popular and loved my life. Then. Now. Always. Even during the time of the Big Hurt. (I'm sounding melodramatic here. But it really was a big hurt and I can still feel it sometimes even today, when I let it wash over me again.)

CHAPTER 3

I liked working for Lockheed Aviation a whole lot more than working at the job, the job I had before that, the one with an undertaker. Picking up the deceased from their homes and helping with the embalming wasn't what I considered a big career move or even a big career, and I was intensely anxious to move upward. (Or at least away from that vocation). Lockheed Aviation offered me that move and I went for it. The people there would at least be alive.

Our family was living on Archwood Street in Van Nuys, a street where many houses were crowded like a crazy quilt into one small area. Directly behind us lived a recently married couple in their fifties, "Doc" (Erwin) and Grace Goddard. They lived in the house owned by Grace's beloved Aunt Ana Lower who lived in West Los Angeles, a woman who was good to them, a woman who would enrich my life, especially during my saddest times. Aunt Ana would figure greatly and with enormous positivity in Norma Jeane's young life, and mine too. She knew Norma Jeane's secrets. I sometimes wish she'd told them, but she did not. She was faithful to Norma Jeane, and she kept those secrets and, I regret to say, died with them.

Doc had brought a young daughter, Bebe, (pronounced "BB") into his marriage with Grace, and she along with the Goddards were very involved with my family, as neighbors who live close together often get to be.

And I became casually aware that they also had another adolescent girl living with them. She was a "charity case," as they called it back then, and she'd just come out of an orphanage, although she wasn't truly an orphan, since her mother was still alive and so probably was her father, although no one knew where he was. Her name was Norma Jeane Mortensen, or Baker, depending on who her mother would decide at any given moment who her father had been, and the Goddards had become her foster parents.

Grace Goddard had worked with Gladys, Norma Jeane's strange mother, and in spite of Gladys's oddnesses, the two had become close friends. But Gladys was an unbalanced woman who regularly went in and out of sanity and in and out of mental institutions, often being taken away under heavy sedation after losing all control, this occurring frequently in front of her frightened little girl.

In one of her rare and more lucid moments, Gladys had finally had the good sense to ask Grace if she'd take Norma Jeane to live with them. The child would be a ward of the state of California, but still, Grace would be paid for taking her, just as foster parents are paid today. Besides, Norma Jeane and their daughter Bebe were about the same age. They would be like sisters. It was settled.

Norma Jeane's last name went back and forth between Mortensen and Baker because Gladys had married both men but was never sure which had fathered her daughter although later it was determined the father was someone else entirely, a film cutter and then director of no fame by the name of C. Stanley Gifford. Norma Jeane's mother Gladys had also been a film cutter in that studio and that apparently, is where Gifford and her mother met.

Norma Jeane never was sure in the beginning who her real father was and it haunted her terribly. I saw how it did. I saw the tears, heard the weeping. I was there when she called him that night. I was there when he cruelly rejected her. I was there.

But I didn't know any of this back then when the Goddards lived close to my family and that there were two young girls always together, playing and laughing. All I knew was that the Goddards had these two kids in their charge, and I knew Bebe was their daughter and the other kid was not. The rumor was that this other kid's mother was still somewhere around, although I understood she was in a mental institution somewhere. I'd heard she was called Norma Jeane something--I wasn't interested in learning her last name. I had a whole lot of other more important things on my mind; girls. Girls certainly a lot older than those two kids at the Goddard's house.

The girls I was interested in back then were more like "women" I used to think, and maybe they were. One of them I actually wanted to marry, but she'd had the very good sense to advise me I couldn't possibly support her in the manner to which she'd like to become accustomed. That knocked me, and badly, but I bounced back quickly, a personality quirk I've always had, if that's what it can be called. Whenever life has delivered me a major blow, I've only staggered a bit and have then gotten straight back into line and have continued on with my life. Perhaps in today's world that would be called "denial." I call calling it that pure BS. It's not denial; it is only good common sense. I have never allowed disappointment or sadness to grip me for long and I simply refuse to waste my energy brooding about spilled milk. I will never let anything pull me in a direction I do not wish to go. Later, when the worst of blows slammed into me, I was able to recover, to lick my wounds for a few moments and to move on, although even today I still feel the pain of that blow. It's still fresh. It still hurts just as much and I know it always will. I just think that whatever hours I have on this earth should not be wasted in moping or worrying or regretting.

But back then, when those two young girls lived with the Goddards near my home, I was nearly twenty and I was still fancy free and happily footloose and had every intention of staying that way for a long time!

My mother and Grace Goddard got to be pretty close, the way people will when their homes are near each other and a back fence is the communication altar. They chatted and gossiped all the time, discussing the world's problems, the neighborhood problems and of course the joys and trials of family life.

And when the Goddards moved to a dilapidated but more spacious home about a mile away on Odessa St., my mother missed Grace's close company, although they quite easily switched the back fence for a telephone.

This new Goddard home, however, posed a transportation problem for the two young girls living with them. They had no way of getting home from Van Nuys High School. It was the fall of 1940.

"Jimmie," said my mother one day. "Grace wants to know if you could drive the girls home from school in the afternoon on your way to work at Lockheed."

"What girls?" I answered.

"You know. Bebe and Norma Jeane. Think you could do that for them?"

I thought about it. I wasn't keen on it, but the Goddards were good friends with my family, so I decided to do the neighborly thing and said, "Well, OK. I'll do it. I won't mind it much, just as long as they're quiet." My mother smiled widely at me, and I remember wondering why.

But even though I'd laid down the law about being quiet, it turned out that the girls weren't. I became extremely incensed one afternoon when those two kids were playing outside my bedroom in the livingroom while I was trying to sleep. They were romping with their spaniel, and squealing happily with absolutely no consideration for my having to sleep just a short distance from them. I'd been working the graveyard shift at Lockheed and very much needed my daytime sleep. I got up from my bed ready to exert my authority, to put the fear of God into them, to show them I was the grown-up here, the guy in charge. The man! I walked to the door.

Norma Jeane was down on the floor, the spaniel jumping all over her and licking her face. She was giggling and shrieking, obviously unable to stop.

"Can the loud noises, you two," I yelled at them. "I'm trying to sleep in here." I have a powerful and naturally deep voice, and used it then to its maximum. After all, I had to show them that I was the adult and that adults are to be obeyed.

Norma Jeane pushed the dog off and sat up. I looked

down at her, summoning up my mature look, in control, angry. She was immediately apologetic and so startlingly sweet----she was downright angelic. There's no other term I can use. At that moment, right then, right there, she completely melted my heart. But I had a serious image to maintain, however, my being a young, popular stud and all, with a car and job and everything, but when she spoke to me with such incredible purity saying she was so awfully sorry she'd awakened me, all I could do was just growl, "Well, don't worry about it. Forget it." And I lay back down. I sure showed them!

And so the routine began of my driving those two young girls home from school every day, and it didn't get past me that Norma Jeane never let Bebe sit in the middle of the seat. Norma Jeane took that place every day, right from the very start, and it was impossible for me to not notice she was pressing close to me, and when she laughed her musical, light laughter, I also couldn't help but notice that her hand would gently touch my knee. And, our daily conversations were becoming more familiar, kind of just for us, to a point where poor Bebe was being left out altogether.

I used to smile indulgently at this eager young kid wanting to be close to me, to talk in a more intimate way. I couldn't really blame her. After all, I was older, much older and far more experienced than these two wet-behind-the-ears young girls. I had a job. I was mature. A big man, important. With a car. And I did happen to notice that Norma Jeane was very beautiful. Luminous sort of. Glowing kind of.

And then Pearl Harbor turned the country upside down and inside out. Everything was different. We were all afraid on some level. But life went on in Van Nuys. I continued to work, and continued to drive Bebe and Norma Jeane home from school every day. Routine was important to everyone then; all of us clung to a semblance of normalcy. It gave us a sense of security, and also meant, we hoped, that life was not going to change, that regular routine would keep us safe, that if we kept up a regular, normal every-day routine we didn't really have to be afraid. But we all gradually did become more and more apprehensive about the future. War changes things. War greatly changes one's thinking, attitudes, and definitely, it changes our dreams.

Doc Goddard's company, Adel Precision Products, held a Christmas dance that year, and during their daily phone forays, Mother and Grace decided it might be nice if I were to take Norma Jeane as my date, and when those two ladies decided something "might be nice," well then, people had better pay attention. What it really translated to was; It Shall Be Done. (I'd really learn that rule later on.) Mom, always the conniver, asked me later on if I would take Norma Jeane to the dance, and oh yes, would I find a date for Bebe, too?

"Well, yeah," I said, hesitating. "I guess that sounds like it might be fun. Maybe. Oh I don't know---" I hesitated, because being the mature young man I was, you know, so much older than Norma Jeane, and of course so much more experienced, I wasn't sure if that was the image I wanted to project to the world, an older guy squiring a kid to a Christmas dance. Well, I sighed and finally decided, I'd show the kid a nice time. I mean after all, it was the least I could do, it being Christmas and all.

Later, I found out that Norma Jeane had been ecstatic when she'd heard the plan. Was it because I was an adult? Let's face it, she was probably excited because I'd become, or so I thought, a very big deal. I could understand the kid's having a hero worship thing for me. Or was she excited about going out with me because we drove home together from high school every day? Or because I drove her there in a prime car for that time--a 1940 Ford Coupe? No. None of that. She was thrilled, as she later told Grace, because I'd been a such a big wheel on the Van Nuys High School campus, with my picture on the wall of the main hall right next to the drama classroom. This impressed Norma Jeane greatly, and of course that Christmas season that this young girl had been absolutely right about my importance. What I didn't know was that the young Norma Jeane Baker was deeply affected and impressed by anyone who had any connection with drama, even if it was only a photograph hanging next to a drama classroom such as I'd had, or a person (me, in this case) who had actually acted in highschool plays.

The dance was wonderful. I was surprised and not unhappy to discover that I was having a marvelous time with this kid, Norma Jeane Mortensen. Baker. Whatever. It didn't matter what her name was. That night there was no way I couldn't notice that she'd lean in very close to me during the slow numbers. I mean very close. She was no kid when she did that. When the band played the sweet "Everything Happens to Me," I could see this pretty girl had her eyes closed as she rested her head against my chest. Grace and Doc, sitting on the sidelines watching us dance, noticed that I'd gone way past doing the neighborly thing and that I was, it was plain for everyone to see, having the time of my life.

But even so, and even though I knew something, some feeling was awakening within me for that young girl, I only asked her out for a couple of casual dates after that. Once to Grauman's Chinese. But she pleased me when we were out together, and young men at nearly twenty years old find it irresistible when a young woman pleases them. We are saps for that and there's not much point in denying it. Norma Jeane laughed when I presumed she was supposed to, and remained quiet when I presumed she was supposed to. I was becoming more and more aware that Norma Jeane was becoming awfully comfortable to be around, really nice company and I was not unaware that I was beginning to look forward to her being beside me each day after school was out.

But still, I couldn't help thinking a lot about how extremely young she was, from my perspective of four more years of experience and worldliness. I began to think I'd better get more serious about dating women my own age, and so I set about doing just that.

Ah, but still, as hard as I tried to resist it, the daily message was becoming clearer by the day; Norma Jeane liked me. I could see it in her expression when she got out of the car, hear it in the gentleness of her words to me, see it in her smile, her warm, tender smile. Was there ever such a smile as that? She glowed when she smiled at me and the very air seemed to get lighter, brighter. There would be this kind of sparkle all around us when Norma Jeane smiled at me. Honestly, I never knew a girl who could smile so dearly, so warmly. I was beginning to realize that this girl/child was awfully grown up for only fifteen.

But all good things, it's said, must come to an end, and my driving the girls home from school finally stopped and the reasons were not good. Quite suddenly, an incident occurred which would forever change my life, and certainly Norma Jeane's too. The very first important steps were about to be taken which would start my Norma Jeane on the not so long path into the life and times of Ms. Marilyn Monroe.

Norma Jeane told me one day that she was going to have to leave the Goddard family because they found they would soon have to move to West Virginia. Sadly, they would be unable to take her along. She was under-age and a ward of the state of California and could not legally move away, even with her foster family. And so, Norma Jeane moved in with Aunt Ana Lower, who was a distant aunt of Grace Goddard's and no relation of Norma Jeane's at all. If that good woman had not taken her in, Norma Jeane would have had to go back to an orphanage, no two ways about it, and it would have killed that sweet flower of a child. She was beginning to blossom and to put her back at age 15 into an orphanage would have damaged her personally and forever. Until she got the news that Aunt Ana would take her in, Norma Jeane was about as depressed and down as a person can be.

Aunt Ana and Norma Jeane had become very close over the past summer. She loved older people and was filled with respect for them, always interested in their families, their histories and I know now that her interest in people's family histories was because her own background left a lot to be desired, although it wasn't as horrifying as the media made it out to be after Norma Jeane became famous. She used to tell me that she truly believed that everyone was good, everyone had some redeeming something about himself or herself. She always insisted that there was goodness in everyone and she wasn't trying to be any kind of a Pollyanna. She really believed that. But sadly, I think that feeling left her after we parted and she became part of the Hollywood jungle. Then, she learned otherwise. Then, she learned the hard way, the hardest. She lost not only her life, but before that, she lost so much of her own, unique magic when she went to Hollywood. She lost her beliefs in the goodness in all people, because out there, she quickly found out that there in fact are lots of people who do not have any innate goodness. She lost so much, my Norma Jeane did. And losing her precious life was an incredibly stupid waste.

CHAPTER 4

It was spring, 1942. We were in the war now for certain. Very much into it; Pearl Harbor had seen to that. I was still working at Lockheed and found myself being occasionally, and sometimes vaguely, puzzled because I found myself really missing those afternoons when I drove Norma Jeane and Bebe home from school.

And then the day came that was to change my life forever. Days always come which change people's lives forever, and I know that's an awful cliche, but for me it was true and I remember it very well. And, like another cliché, I remember it "as if it were yesterday." And I do. I've had many "epiphany" days, but this one I'll carry with me until I die.

The new course of my life began that day in early spring when my mother called me aside and asked a question. Several questions.

"Jimmie," she said.

"Yeah?"

"I want to ask you a kind of favor--a favor involving Norma Jeane."

"I'm listening."

"Well, you know she had to move in with Grace's Aunt Ana because Grace and Doc had to move to West Virginia. They could take Bebe, but they couldn't take Norma Jeane. Remember? It was illegal for Norma Jeane to go to leave California 'cause she's a ward of the state, or something like that, and she'd have had to go to an orphanage and ..."

"Yeah. Of course, Mom. I remember." I could hear a slight edge to my voice. (Sometimes it was advisable to cut my mother off before she got too much on a roll.

"Well Jimmie, Aunt Ana--she's a dear, and a wonderful woman who has been so good to the Goddards..."

"Yeah," I said, beginning to get impatient. "I know all this. Where's this goin', Mom?"

"Well Jimmie, poor little Norma Jeane, that sweet, darlin' girl, well, Aunt Ana is just too old to look after her and now it looks as if Norma Jeane will have to go back to the orphanage she was in a few years ago. Awful things, orphanages, doncha think?"

"I guess they are. She will?"

"Yes. And so," said my mother who could occasionally get straight to the point when she realized it was the best thing to do under the circumstances, "Well Jimmie, Grace wanted to know if you would be interested in marrying Norma Jeane."

I stared at her.

"Mom, she's a fifteen year old kid!"

"Yes Jimmie--that's the whole point. By law she's too young to be out on her own. Like I said before, she's a ward of the state, you know? But if she were a married lady, then she wouldn't have to go back to the orphanage. I've heard they're such awful places. Really bad. Have you heard that too?"

I could feel myself being had--but surprised that I really didn't mind. Not at all. I was actually sort of feeling good about this very sudden, very weird idea. But, I continued to stare at my mother.

The idea of marrying Norma Jeane had never occurred to me. Not once, even during those few dates, during the times she moved so close to me in the car on those afternoons, when we danced together that night, when she spoke so softly to me, caringly, smiled so warmly, sweetly. No. Never once. And besides, she was so young and everything and I was so mature. With a job. And a car. Remember?

Continuing to look at my mother, I knew right away. My heart and my head told me I just could not possibly let Norma Jeane go back to the orphanage if I could save her from that. I felt obligated. Someone had to step in and rescue this beautiful, sweet girl, this young maiden. Someone like one of those knights in shining armor I'd read about as a kid. A knight sort of like, well, …me. What else could I do? I said yes. After all, it was the only decent thing a gentleman could do, under the circumstances.

Without missing a beat my mother said "Let's set it up for June." And then I knew it was something that had been in the works for a while between those two women and even as young and inexperienced as I was, I knew I, like all men everywhere, hadn't stood a chance. The battle and the war had been won long before I'd been approached.

Thus, It was a done deal. Norma Jeane would be sixteen on June first. It was time for me to start courting her.

Sometimes I'd take her hiking in the Hollywood hills, but one of our favorite things to do was to go was boating at a small place in the hills called Pop's Willow Lake. It was a perfect setting for lovers, and we'd quite quickly become lovers in whatever sense you may choose to think. Norma Jeane and I would rent a canoe at night and paddle to a place where there were low tree branches to hide us. The lake was lit by floodlights so we weren't ever as completely hidden as we'd have liked, but we could hear music playing from somewhere and it sailed gently across the lake toward us, like magical music from a magical kingdom. It was so beautiful there. We could paddle softly around that lake and talk, learn about, and teach each other. No one can possibly know how surreal and beautiful she looked by lake moonlight back then. She was like morning dew and poured silver. She literally took my breath away. I'd stare at her, at her lovely, lush body, her curly, dark blond hair. She was like a luminous painting in that setting. You think you know from seeing photographs of her at that age, but you don't. No one knows how Norma Jeane looked by moonlight from the sky and reflected from the lake's dark, shining surface. But I do. I was blessed to see that sight. I can't forget it.

One night as we were parked on the wickedly infamous Mullholland Drive looking at the lights below us, the radio, which had been playing Glenn Miller's famous theme song,

"Moonlight Serenade," suddenly went dead. I reached for the knob but couldn't get the radio to go again and I grumbled because it had been such a sweet moment, sitting there with Norma Jeane's beautiful head resting against my shoulder, that wonderful music playing.

"It doesn't matter, Honey," she whispered up at me. And she hummed the rest of the tune for me. Her voice was sweet and light and she sang right on key. It thrilled me to hear her sing like that and made me think that we'd be able to spend a lot of time singing after we were married. Music was very important to me back then, and I'd been entertaining people with my own singing for many years. I loved the sound of Norma Jeane's sweet, clear voice in my car that night. She made me feel so alive and happy, and that is another dear memory she's left me with.

I hated to break the mood, but had to. "Norma Jeane, sweetheart, I'm awfully sorry, but I think we're in trouble, Darlin'. What time do you have to be home?"

"Eleven o'clock. You know Grace."

I did know Grace and knew we'd better get back by eleven or there'd be hell to pay. I also knew my car and understood if the radio went dead, the car wouldn't start, at least not in the usual way. I'd had this experience before with it.

I pushed Norma Jeane's head gently from my chest and began to explain to her how I'd have to shove the car down the hill while she sat behind the wheel to hold the clutch in. Norma Jeane sat up and yawned.

"OK, Honey," she said. "I can do that for you." I got out of the car and she slid over to the steering wheel.

"Now Norma Jeane, I'll push the car, you hold that clutch in and when I tell you, let it out and step on the gas. That'll get the motor running and when that happens, you can put on the brake. Got it?"

"I got it, Jimmie." She stretched slowly and yawned widely again. "You can count on me."

I shoved the car hard and it began to roll and I shouted "Let go of the clutch, Norma Jeane!" and she did. And then, as she'd been instructed, she stepped on the gas--but she seemed to forget the part about putting on the brake and the car began to pick up speed. I was galloping alongside, and all the training I'd had in sports was very helpful at that moment because I was running faster than I ever had in my life! But the car was going too fast and the distance between us was rapidly widening.

"The brake! The brake!" I was screaming, losing my breath and watching the back of the car get farther and farther away. Finally, Norma Jeane found the brake and slammed it on hard and the car jolted and screeched to a stop, leaving thick black streaks on the road. I slammed on my brakes too, puffing loudly. I could hardly stand up. I was about a block away and walked up to the car, sucking in huge gulps of air. I looked inside and found Norma Jeane having an hysterical fit of laughter. I mean, she was doubled over on herself and the mirth poured from her and her beautiful, nearly shut blue eyes.

"Oh Jimmie," she gasped. "The sight of you charging down that hill after me was the funniest thing I think I've ever seen. Ever!" She could hardly get the words out she was laughing so fiercely. "You should enter the Olympics, Honey! You were running so, so fast!" and she again began laughing until she was nearly out of control.

I stood leaning into the window, my breath calming, but only somewhat. "Yeah, right. It was a riot," I growled at her, making every effort to show my anger. It had no effect on Norma Jeane—it made her laugh all the more.

"Move over, Norma Jeane," I said gruffly. "I've got to get you home." I was having trouble keeping my mature composure. She pulled her knees up under her chin and wrapped her arms around them and continued to shriek with laughter all the way home.

And we did get her home before eleven. Playing by the rules was always very important to Norma Jeane. She knew she had to toe the mark with Grace and also with Aunt Ana. It was never Norma Jeane's style to cross either of those women or to fail at doing everything she was asked. Norma

Jeane (Baker) (Mortensen) was a good girl, in every sense. I want the world to know this about her; she had ethics and a great sense of right and wrong. She was honest and had a purity about her I'd never seen before in anyone, and in few people since we parted.

And Norma Jeane could also be very reserved and circumspect, keeping things in gentle restraint during our courtship.

"Jim's such a wonderful person," I was told she once confided to Grace. "I want to marry him. I really do. I love Jim, but I don't know anything about sex. Can we get married without having sex?"

"Don't worry about that," Grace advised the young, worried girl. "Jim will teach you." And that seemed to calm her uneasiness. Norma Jeane trusted me. She knew then and knew always that I'd never hurt her. I never knowingly did, I never did on purpose and I never wanted to. But my Norma Jeane was a tender plant and I know I hurt her sometimes. She'd been hurt so much in her short life and it had never toughened her or made her strong. When people took aim at her in order to cause her pain, they usually hit their mark, and for all of her too short life, Norma Jeane was a very easy mark.

CHAPTER 5

The date of our wedding was drawing nearer and Norma Jeane and I were getting more excited about it every day. We talked and planned and dreamed constantly. It was a wonderful time for us where we could be completely selfish, thinking only of ourselves. We were falling more and more in love and to describe our feelings for each other as "delirious" can't even touch how we felt. We laughed and sometimes wept with joy. She was genuinely happy about our coming marriage, full of newer and newer plans, and full of love for me. And I for her.

Just as Grace and my mother had hoped, we fell in love almost immediately when our marriage was "decided" by those two sly women. Maybe it happened when I began to court her. And of course, maybe I'd loved her from the start, but hadn't known, being such a bigshot, so popular with the girls, and so much older and everything. And with a car.

But there was a cloud over my Norma Jeane--not a big one, but there it was anyway. She'd had a lot of profound respect for Grace Goddard, and Grace was leaving her behind, the way she'd been left behind so often in her fifteen years of life. Los Angeles County had seen to it that Norma Jeane was quickly placed in foster homes and orphanages often while her mother Gladys floated in and out of mental institutions. There was no father to protect her, to save her, to keep her in a safe place and a safe home. No father for her, ever. Until I came along. I was so young then and didn't realize fully the meaning of her love and need for me. But as I've aged and studied on this, I realize that while she did love me as a lover and friend and husband, there was something about the father image thing too. And that's OK. There's nothing so terribly sinister and sick about that in my opinion. People make much of it, but so what if in the mix there's a father need? We were passionate lovers and believe me, when we were making love, I wasn't being at all fatherly!

Norma Jeane tried not to, but she couldn't help but consider the Goddard's leaving her behind was yet another rejection, even though she understood their position. Intellectually she knew they had to go because of Doc's income concerns, but emotionally she felt once again as if she were being abandoned, that she was being left to fend for herself, to be unprotected, to be left vulnerable and unsafe once again, and it hurt her heart and soul.

Norma Jeane also understood the circumstances of her coming nuptials, that she was offered marriage with me to keep her from having to go to yet another orphanage, and so she was grateful to me and my mother and Grace for setting the wedding up. And happily, it was from the start a pleasant and happy experience, a thrilling time for us in many, many ways.

And so you see, the problem for my Norma Jeane was a pretty simple one; when Grace had taken her out of the orphanage and offered her a home with them, she'd promised Norma Jeane she'd never have to suffer with that kind of life again. Thus, when the Goddards had to move to West Virginia, Norma Jeane, although she truly tried not to think like this, understanding that they just had to go, felt that Grace had gone back on her word. She always had a very big problem with people who did not keep their promises. But then of course, the time came when she herself didn't keep one; the most important one, at least to me.

Norma Jeane was in love with me and let me know always that I made her happy. But I guess I'll always wonder if in the way-back of her mind, in the quiet, secret place she kept hidden from me and eventually the world, she was afraid I too would leave her, abandon her, make her go back to all the places she was frightened of. Did Norma Jeane spend her life leaving people before they had a chance to leave her? Was this a pattern developed from her old childhood fears? I learned that because she was so afraid of certain things from her childhood, it was so hard to make those scary and painful shadows go away. So hard. And for her I think they never did. Norma Jeane was chased by those shadows all of her life, and even during our very short and very happy time together.

At the time of our planned nuptials, Norma Jeane was attending University High School in Los Angeles, and apparently spoke freely and happily with her new classmates about her forthcoming marriage, telling them proudly she was going to drop out of high school that very year, in her eleventh, or junior, year.

I smiled when she told me she said these things. The little girl named Norma Jeane that I knew was very protective about her private life, extremely secretive. But now she was suddenly telling everyone who'd listen to her what her new plans were. She very well knew that these plans were startling to most people, especially older ones, and she loved the excitement she was causing. After all, she was very young--not even sixteen yet, and she was going to be a wife. I couldn't help wondering about the side of her that seemed to enjoy shocking people — she clearly did enjoy doing that!

I remember Norma Jeane's telling me about her social studies teacher's reaction to the news of her coming marriage.

"He told me I'd be ruining my life," she giggled. "But Jimmie, I told him I knew exactly what I was doing and about much I loved you. And you know what he said? He said that at not quite sixteen, it was doubtful I knew what love really is. A lot he knows, Jimmie. I know exactly what love is." And I think, because of her love-deprived background, she did know on some level what love really is--or at least what it is not. I could not disapprove of Norma Jeane's wanting to tell the world about her new life, her "catch." If I tried to be stern with her, telling her it was "unseemly" for her to brag to the world about this upcoming event, she melted me down with her smile, the way she always did.

That teacher's warning flew past her and disappeared. I was now the only thing in Norma Jeane's life, her only future, and there was no room for anything else.

I remember during our courtship when Aunt Ana told me confidentially that Norma Jeane had told her she couldn't really believe that anyone like me who'd been so "popular with the girls" would ever settle for her, and that she couldn't also believe how special I made her feel. And I worked at that, making her feel special, having fallen hopelessly in love with this golden child. Even back then, before we were married and afterwards too, I worked at making Norma Jeane understand how desirable she was, how worthy she was of anyone's respect and admiration, and certainly their love. I knew she was needy and frightened, afraid to turn her back on people she loved, afraid she'd turn around and they'd be gone. I knew she was unable to trust, that because she found herself so often and so suddenly without a mother, that she could not really trust people. I knew she always wondered as soon as she made a new friend, "will this one leave me too?"

CHAPTER 6

Norma Jeane and I finally decided on a place for our marriage ceremony. It would be at the home of Chester Howell of Westwood, a friend of the Goddards.

"Oh Jimmie," Norma Jeane one day said breathlessly to me. "I'm so happy they'll let us get married there because they've got that winding staircase coming into their front hall. What's that called again? A spiral? Yeah! Oh, it'll be so romantic and perfect! Just like in the movies, Jimmie! Just like!" I smiled down at her. I knew how much Norma Jeane loved movies, how excited she became over movie stars, even the unglamorous ones, but never once did I ever get the slightest hint from her that she had any unusual fancy for movies, or any special or secret dreams about maybe being in them.

Norma Jeane took a very active interest in all our wedding plans and during that time, I began to realize I was falling more and more in love with this unusual young girl, and happier by the day that my mother and Grace had decided our fates the way they had. It seemed a century ago when I was "out in the world" chasing the girls, showing everyone what a stud I was, with a job and a car and everything. Now I was committed to this luminous, young bride-to-be and I did not miss those (not so) old days one bit.

But oddly, I learned during this time that Norma Jeane hadn't yet realized how deeply I had begun to love her and that she'd begun to worry I might be taking this big step with her out of some sense of duty or kindness on my part. Or out of obligation.

"He's so kind," she used to tell people, including my own mother. "Jimmie's really just too good. I sometimes get afraid that people will take advantage of his good nature." But she would finally come to know shortly after our marriage that it was no act of noble kindness that compelled me to marry her. My astonishing Norma Jeane had offered me her heart, only me, and I often felt humbled at the gift. I remember thinking that no one else would have her heart but I. We would belong to each other for eternity.

As our time together progressed, I began, to my delight, to notice that Norma Jeane wanted to be with me all the time, every possible moment. Before our wedding, she even wanted to start living in the Archwood house with my mother.

But I did not at all want her to move in with Mother and so distracted Norma Jeane from this plan by taking her apartment hunting. And as we went through this phase of our courtship, I learned even more good things about her. I recall when we found a brand new studio apartment on Vista del Monte in Sherman Oaks we wanted to rent as man and wife, Norma Jeane was transported with joy. The landlords told us that if we promised to stay for six months, they'd purchase a new couch for us, and Norma Jeane assured them we would. She was just simply ecstatic about the place and told me it was the very first time in her entire life she would have a home of her own and she just couldn't wait to begin being my wife and a "home owner." The apartment had a Murphy pull-down bed that quite simply thrilled and delighted her. She was like a kid at Christmas, and all I could do was just watch all of this happen and stand around grinning a lot. She did make me very happy.

The new landlords accepted Norma Jeane without question as a bride-to-be, even though she was obviously so very young. But Norma Jeane Baker was quite mature for her age, and most certainly had a mature woman's body, and so could carry it off. She was also terribly proper, a trait she either inherited from her mother Gladys or had observed and copied from Grace or Aunt Ana. (Or maybe from watching the glamorous, proper ladies in the endless movies she'd been sent to as a small child, to fill up her hours.) There was nothing of the giddy, silly teenager about her. When you were with Norma Jeane, you knew you were with a very special person, a very special woman. I loved her so much I sometimes thought my heart would burst. She was everything to me----my life, my reason for being, and my most miraculous joy.

On June 19, 1942, and 18 days into her sixteenth year, Norma Jeane Mortensen (or Baker) became my wife. I won't forget that wonderful day when she made me happier than I could have ever thought possible. I sometimes think about it, although my life today is extremely happy and I do not often mourn the loss of Norma Jeane. Not too much, that is. Sometimes. I guess when you've been dealt a miracle in your life, you are grateful and you don't forget, and you shouldn't mourn its passing because miracles like everything else pass on. I think we should rejoice in their happening, because they're not given to everyone. I don't know why I was one of the Chosen, but I was. But, Norma Jeane was not the only miracle in my life. I've been dealt many in my life, and a great many of them happened after we parted.

Reverend Benjamin Lingenfelder officiated at the ceremony. He'd been close to our family since I was a small boy, and had been instrumental in teaching me to be a good shot with a rifle and shotgun. Reverend Lingenfelder was a minister in the Christian Science Church and performed the ceremony from that faith. Norma Jeane had chosen the Christian Science faith as her own also, and I had lapsed into non-attendance in the Catholic Church, so this was fine with me.

A high school classmate of Norma Jeane's served as maid of honor and my brother Marion was best man. My young nephew Wes Kanteman was ring bearer. Norma Jeane wore a pure white, long silken dress, with a short veil attached to her thick, curly hair. It was a borrowed dress, but that didn't matter to either of us. I know that there has never been a more beautiful bride. I wanted to laugh and I wanted to weep, but I did neither. I just stared at this creature floating down that spiral staircase toward me in that dress, looking like an angel, smiling straight at me, me, me; her whole focus was me, my whole focus was her. I thought my heart would burst. I heard a piano playing the wedding march. Who was that playing? I don't remember.

It was a short ceremony without too many in the gathering; some buddies from work and their girlfriends. Aunt Ana was there as well as Norma Jeane's very first foster parents, the Albert Bolenders, who had come up from Hawthorne for the ceremony. But if it had been a huge wedding in the biggest church in the world with everyone everywhere standing watching, I could not have been more thrilled and excited. This remarkable, enchanting young girl was my wife, for all of my life. Even after all the planning, after everything, I still could not believe my good fortune. I am an emotional person, and when we spoke our promises to each other that wonderful day, it touched me in the deepest part of my soul. My bliss, my elation was Norma Jeane's too. We were one. I no longer knew where I ended and she began. I'd never known happiness like this.

Norma Jeane had done her own hair for her special day and it looked beautiful, glossy, and curly. She always had told me that "I'm the only one who can curl my hair the way I want it." I remember looking at the soft, light brown ringlets and I touched the curls that tumbled from beneath her veil.

I know we spoke our vows to each other and I remember her voice was soft and sweet, a little scared. We stared at each other, and I thought I'd drown in her eyes. I don't remember the words said over us during the ceremony. I do remember having her next to me, seeing her, smelling her, dazzled by her beauty. I remember how Norma Jeane looked up at me after the ceremony was completed and smiled her huge, sweet smile. It said to me "I trust you. I believe what you say. I love you." That smile could have melted stone and I'll never forget how she looked at just that moment. Her beautiful eyes were so expressive. I could not believe how lucky I was and thought no man ever could have been so happy, so in love. No man.

After the ceremony, I took everyone to a party at the

Florentine Gardens in Hollywood. Norma Jeane wore a pale blue suit that fit her beautiful young body perfectly. She wore high heels but even so, the top of her head came just to my shoulder, and that day her head stayed very close to my shoulder!

To my surprise, I discovered on our wedding day how very jealous my new bride could be. There was a show going on at the Florentine Gardens the day of our reception, and one of the professional dancers up on the stage asked me, the new groom, to come up and dance with her. I did it immediately while everyone clapped and cheered and laughed. I was having a wonderful time until I looked down on the floor and into Norma Jeane's face. She was not enjoying my performance at all! She was angry and jealous and obviously very upset. I stopped the dance immediately and came back down to the new Mrs. Dougherty, and she was happy again, and I assured her I would never do that again!

I kept my white tuxedo jacket on for the party and a waiter had the very poor judgment to spill spaghetti sauce on it, but I didn't get my Irish up. After all, it was my wedding day and I didn't want to spoil it by punching the guy. He didn't mean to I know, but the jacket, of course, was ruined. But, I will admit to being astonished when he asked me for a tip at the end of the day. You've gotta admire a guy like that!

Everyone commented on how happy and excited Norma Jeane was on that day, her day, my day--our day. And except to go to the bathroom, she never let go of my arm for the entire time, constantly looking up at me as if she were afraid I might disappear forever. I never would do that to her, and always promised her I'd be with her forever. But there many fears locked deep in that little girl's heart, and I knew about all of them. Or I thought I did. People she'd loved before had disappeared and she'd never gotten over the sense of abandonment. I was determined to give my beautiful new wife everything in the world she needed. For as long as we both shall live.

CHAPTER 7

Our life together began without fanfare; quietly, even gently. I went back to work at Lockheed the Monday following our wedding, and had to suffer through the usual kidding friends and fellow workers heap on one another after a wedding. Norma Jeane and I never had a honeymoon in the sense of flying to Bermuda or Niagara Falls. We just couldn't afford it, but our being together for that weekend was enough, and my memory of that time with her is clear and strong and with me.

When I was back at work, I know my fellow workers saw the delighted look on my face when I found a little note in my lunchbox. My dear, darling new wife wrote that she would be dreaming of me while I worked. (I was still on the graveyard shift and she'd be home in bed, asleep, waiting for me.)

I was only twenty-one, but was old enough to recognize what real love was. But sometimes, because I was so young, I felt a slight apprehension because of the sense of responsibility I'd taken on with a new wife. Norma Jeane was a fragile girl in many ways, frightened of loss, and with the Goddards gone for good and her mother Gladys yet again in another institution, I was all Norma Jeane had. She had her beloved Aunt Ana, too, but I was her whole life. And I loved that, loved how she needed me. My feelings for Norma Jeane Dougherty were very deep and amazingly strong. But still I sometimes felt overwhelmed with the responsibility of caring for this child bride of mine. Sure, I know thousands and thousands of people have married very young and have had remarkably long and happy marriages, so we weren't all that unique. I just occasionally felt a bit overawed by this lovely person who'd come into my life.

Ah but then, I was a young, cocky bridegroom, and quite possessive of my new bride, as young, cocky bridegrooms often are. But as things turned out, I was amazed to learn I was no more possessive of her than she was of me. I recall how we once went to a lodge at Big Bear, a skiing resort, where we skied and played in the snow together like children. I wish the world could have seen her rolling and jumping in the snow like that--glistening, laughing, her bright smile closely matching the sun on the snow. Sometimes when I'd see Norma Jeane like that, my heart would ache with love for her. She glowed all the time, but playing in the snow...well, it was something shimmering, magical. I'll never forget it and no photograph of her since then has ever matched the beauty of that sight.

Norma Jeane had a natural proficiency for certain sports, and skiing was one of them. She was able to stay upright almost immediately on the beginner's slopes and soon graduated to the steeper hills. We had a wonderful time together when we skied and it's quite a feeling being on skis and flying behind a girl who looked the way Norma Jeane looked in the snow.

But the war, from the American standpoint, was really on by that winter of 1942, and because all men had been drafted, there was only one other man besides myself at the lodge. He was a big, handsome Norwegian merchant seaman. He and I were not unaware that the lodge was filled with at least twenty young women who were happily anxious to occupy our time. We really could not have avoided these ladies unless we'd locked ourselves in our rooms, and there was no way we were gonna do that! He and I began to play poker with all the women, who made a great clucking, giggling fuss over our wizardry at the game. We played for an hour or more when Norma Jeane suddenly stormed out and ran upstairs to our room.

I played one more hand and then excused myself and hurried upstairs. I found her curled on our bed, weeping nearly uncontrollably.

"Darlin'," I said, sitting next to her and stroking her hair.

"Why are you crying, Sweetheart?"

"Jimmie," she said through her tears, "I have to know this-- why are you wasting your time with all those girls down there when you've got me for company? I'm your wife. Isn't that enough for you now?"

It was enough. More than enough, and I was instantly sorry I'd made her feel so left out, ignored. I pulled her into my arms.

"You're right, Norma Jeane. Why indeed should I?"

"Jimmie," she went on, calmed now, "I just don't think this is the way a couple in love should spend a weekend to- gether." I held her tightly and rocked her. And for the rest of that weekend, I spent every minute with my new bride, leaving the entire harem to the elated sailor. Norma Jeane, as she always had, just simply knocked me out with her very uncomplicated outlook on the way people in love were expected to behave, and this way of looking at life, so clear and innocent, so logical and seemingly right, made me love her more dearly than ever before. My wife pleased me greatly.

There was much learning and teaching we had to go through together, as all young newlyweds must. Norma Jeane was so devoted to me and I sometimes, not too often, but occasionally, took that love for granted.

I remember how often she told me that she was just blown away by the ease with which I handled people. Strangers al- ways terrified her and she said she longed to have the confi- dence I had with the public. She flattered me often, telling me how impressed she still was over my high school accom- plishments, how all the teachers had always had such good things to say about me. Norma Jeane made me feel by her words and actions that I had given her the biggest favor of her life by marrying her. Perhaps that was true for her. I know her marrying me was the biggest favor anyone had ever given me in my life.

CHAPTER 8

Norma Jeane, born on June 1, 1926, was a Gemini.

I'd like it known that I am not a follower of stars or planets, and I'm not completely sure what the difference is between astrology and astronomy. But there was something eerily accurate about the definition of a Gemini with regard to my new wife. Geminis are supposed to be moody, unpredictable and sometimes a little scary. Dual personalities. Twins. These things were all true about Norma Jeane, and I tried to understand, and think to some degree I did. And now when I think of how she turned out, and who she became, I'm nearly certain the twin stars had something to do with all of this. Maybe. Who knows? These things have been around far longer than I have!

As young as I was back then, I understood I was now married to a somewhat damaged young woman who had been unloved for much of her short life and unwanted for too many years, her tender, formative years. These happenings can have a deep effect on anyone, but on a very young and uncommonly sensitive girl, they can be devastating. I could see glimpses of these darker, frightened sides of Norma Jeane and I anguished for her and tried hard to help her through these difficult times, to convince her in every way I was able to that she was adored, respected, and very, very wanted, and that she could trust me utterly. And I think now that of all those, "trust" was highest in importance to her. If she discovered that she'd be unable to trust a person, she kept away from him or her. Norma Jeane was always too frightened to invest a lot of time and effort into someone who might end in leaving her. How awful it must have been for her to be so afraid of that all the time. Honestly it affected her whole life and governed so many of her big life decisions, as tragically short as that life was. Lord, I miss her.

Let me try to give some examples here of the subtle but very evident differences in the personality of this lady I loved. One Saturday we'd gone shopping in one of the small towns in the San Fernando Valley. We parked in an area marked out for rows of cars in front of the stores. I was feeling a little frisky that day and had a silly idea.

"Hey, Norma Jeane," I said. "Let's have a little fun."

"Sure, Jimmie," she said. She looked so pretty that day in a red and white dress, a red ribbon holding back her thick, glossy hair. I can still remember the scent of her light perfume. She grinned at me and as ever, I nearly melted at the sight. She had an endlessly sweet affect on me. I pulled her face to me and kissed her.

"God, you're so gorgeous, Norma Jeane," I said. She giggled. "Hey! What fun do you want to have?" she asked me.

I leaned back. "Tell you what. Wouldn't it be funny if we waited for some guy to walk by and honked the horn while I ducked down and left you sitting there alone?"

"Jimmie, you're kidding!" She looked at me, wide eyed, and then she giggled again. "Well--yeah," she said. "That'd be kinda funny. Let's do it!" She became excited like a little girl about to do some mischief. "Hey look! Here comes a man now. Get down in the back Jimmie--quick!"

I jumped into the back and ducked down. Norma Jeane tapped a few times on the horn. The man stopped, bent and looked through the windshield and saw my beautiful wife sitting there.

"Hi," he said. Norma Jeane smiled back at him and said "Hi," in her sweet, gentle voice. Then the man walked up to the open side window, leaned in and said in a very interested voice, "How y'doin'?"

Norma Jeane's voice got very breathy when she said back to him, "I'm fine," and she drew out the "fine" to a couple of beats longer than necessary, I thought. She said it sort of huskily. Where'd she learn to do that?

I couldn't see him, but I was dead certain that guy was

about to open the car door and get in with my wife. I shot up from the floor in the back. The guy straightened abruptly and looked very startled. He moved quickly away from the car, turned once to look back and then ran away down the street.

I climbed back into the front seat and looked at Norma Jeane. She'd begun to laugh and I knew she was laughing at my foolishness and I also knew she had played the game too well. I could not help myself---I was left with the uneasy sensation that if I hadn't been there in the car, perhaps she would have carried the game father than I would have liked to know. It took a long time for me to shake that feeling, and I've wondered, over the years, if she was inadvertently showing me something about herself that I was too young and too much in love to really notice. And as it turned out, it actually was something she'd later develop and nurture and make work for her. And make work very well, too. When she changed into "her," she had that ability or gift or whatever it was honed to a faretheewell.

Norma Jeane and I stayed in that little apartment for the six months, long enough to get that new couch, and were finally able to move into our first little detached house on Bessemer Street in Van Nuys. Norma Jeane was very happy there, in her first real altogether house. Her own home. She was like a little girl playing house.

One Saturday night we were having a small tiff because she wanted to go out. I was so tired and begged off and we went to bed a little angry with one another. But I fell asleep anyway. I'm a pretty good sleeper and even a row with the woman I loved wasn't going to keep me from getting my ZZZs. After all, I was a working man and had to sleep hard and eat well!

Some time during that night, Norma Jeane got up and left the house wearing only her nightgown. I never heard her leave. I didn't hear her return. But I awakened suddenly to find her holding onto me tightly and crying very hard. I could see the tears drenching her face, her nightgown.

"Norma Jeane, honey, what's the matter?" I reached for

her, nearly shouting.

"Oh Jimmie," she howled, a near scream. "There's a man after me. There's a man after me!" She was hysterical, frantic, and was holding me tightly, her nails digging into my back, my arms. I held her close to me and felt her dreadful sobs shuddering through her body. I rocked her for some minutes.

"Honey," I said softly, wanting to calm her. "Please. Don't cry. You're OK. You're having a nightmare."

She pushed away from me, her face wet, shining with her tears. "No Jimmie. It's true. I'm awake. I'm not having a nightmare! We had that fight and I was gonna leave home, leave you forever, and so I left the house and walked down the street and a man chased me home." She pushed her face against my chest and began to cry again.

"You what?" I shouted, shoving her away from me. "You've got to be crazy. God only knows what that man would've done to you if he'd caught you. Oh my God, Norma Jeane--sure someone's gonna chase you home, you in that nightgown in the middle of the night. Are you completely out of your skull?"

Norma Jeane stiffened suddenly, and became suddenly very quiet. Her tears stopped, her crying stopped, and she let go of me abruptly. It was as if the air had been knocked out of her utterly. I was speechless when that happened, and after some minutes, she slid down under the covers and turned away from me. I don't know if either of us slept that night and the next day, she was subdued, obviously ashamed of herself for what she'd done. But she did not have to be ashamed, and I as I pondered on what had happened, I finally realized that her being withdrawn and pulling away from me was because I'd called her "crazy." I felt badly ashamed, knowing that word had touched a very raw, very hidden part of her, and I vowed I would never, ever call her that again, no matter what the circumstances. I never did. It took a lot of loving and comforting to reassure Norma Jeane when she fell into those moods of hers, but I know I was successful doing that for her. I remember. Many people over the years saw her moods, her mood swings. It made a lot of people very angry, especially those who were paying to keep film people on deck while Norma Jeane, Marilyn Monroe, took those huge emotional dives she took, followed by dark withdrawals. What they didn't know was that she couldn't help it, my poor little darling girl. Anything could trigger them off, and no one, not even she, knew what those things were. If only I'd been there, I could have helped, explained, seen her through those awful things....

I lived with two Norma Jeanes in our new little home on Vista del Monte, just like the sign of the Gemini promises. One was a young child, scared, unable or maybe unwilling to grow up, to become a woman. This child kept dolls propped up on a chest of drawers, "so they can see what's going on," she'd always say. She was so serious when she said that to me, so I never made fun of her, never teased or laughed at her because I understood that for too long, those stuffed creatures had been her only family, the family who didn't leave her, abandon her, or make her afraid. I remember the array; when she'd been very young as a foster child with the Bolender family, she owned the two ceramic cry-baby dolls on the chest. There was a stuffed teddy bear with only one eye, and also stuffed monkey whose tail had disappeared long before. Bebe had once given her a "French" decorator doll, designed to sit on a bed, but since our bed folded up into the wall, it couldn't go there. Finally, there were two rag dolls, and those were Norma Jeane's favorites. She held and loved them, and spoke with them frequently in a sweet, tiny voice. I have often wondered what became of Norma Jeane's "babies," her beloved doll collection. Did she take them with her into her new persona? Did they give her courage and strength when she felt alone and frightened? Were they in the room with her at the end when she lay all alone on that bed? Did they watch in silent, helpless despair when she sighed and died? Were they the last things she saw before she closed her beautiful eyes forever? I wonder what became of her dolls. I wish I had them. I'd get them to her somehow—leave them at her grave---something…

The other Norma Jeane was the very grown up housewife. One of the things which stabs me with guilt occasionally is my remembering how Norma Jeane wanted a child and how I'd talked her out of it. I thought it was too soon. I worried that if I was called and had to fight in World War II and I died, Norma Jeane would be left alone at a terribly young age with a baby to care for, a baby who might have to suffer in foster homes if Norma Jeane were unable to care for it. I was very young myself then, too, and like all young people, I had strong, unshakable opinions, and I told Norma Jeane we would have to wait to start a family.

"Oh Jimmie," she'd say to me, her voice sad and soft. "I guess you're right, but I so would like to start now. But you're wise and a good person. You know best. I'll wait, Jimmie. We'll have a lot of kids when we're both a little older." And she'd smile up at me, but it was a smile filled with sadness. She wanted babies so she could pour love all over them, the way she'd never had it poured over her as a tiny child, the way she poured it over her dolls, over other people's children, the way she poured it over dogs and cats.

After we made the decision to wait, Norma Jeane went to see a doctor and got fitted for a diaphragm so she would not get accidentally pregnant. There was no way she would ever have "tricked" me into becoming a father. Norma Jeane was too straight with me, too honest to ever do anything like that. When she got home, she ran into the bathroom to insert it, as eagerly as if she were going to try on and model a new bathing suit for me. She was going to do the right thing. We'd have our kids later, she said, even if we had to adopt them. Definitely! She seemed resigned. I felt relief. I felt guilt.

I'd rationalize over and over to myself, telling myself that I really feared, back then, if she'd had kids too early, and had to face the responsibility of a family, she might have flipped out like her wacked-out mother did. It was a very real fear for me. I wanted her to grow up first. I maybe wanted to grow up too. Children had every right to expect maturity, strength and security in their parents. We weren't ready.

"We're not taking any chances," Norma Jeane would say bravely to our friends when they mentioned our not having any children. "Things are too unsettled for us right now." Norma Jeane was dignified and calm about it even though I knew how much her heart ached for kids. I was so incredibly proud of the way she handled this issue, with such maturity and poise. I told her that. I wanted her to know how proud she always made me. On a daily basis, I made sure Norma Jeane knew how important she was and how much I adored and respected her.

Norma Jeane Mortensen had known absolutely nothing about sex when she married me. Truly nothing at all, except for what her girlfriends had told her, what they'd giggled about, looked up in books and magazines. My mother had cautioned me about her, telling me she was a virgin and that I should be very careful of her on our first night together. I remember that sweet night. We were both gentle with each other, and it was very obvious that Norma Jeane's "delicate threshold" had never been crossed over before. There was some pain, but I was aware of it and sensitive to her, and after that small discomfort, Norma Jeane just fell crazily in love with sex. I was one lucky man!

I think back to that awful, lurid and sick story, told by Marilyn Monroe herself, that she'd been raped at around eleven or twelve, by a relative. It just simply never could have happened. Our first night together was absolute proof of that. She was a virgin on our wedding night. I'll never understand why Marilyn Monroe said those things, unless someone advised her to, someone who convinced her she'd be more famous if people heard stories like that, that she'd garner more attention, headlines and renown if she told those sorts of tales. I would someday like to know the answers to these questions, to know why she did and said those things every time she lost herself and became the other woman, Marilyn, an occurrence which happened so much she became Marilyn completely and lost Norma Jeane to the ages. Someday, of course, I'll have the answers. I know I shall.

What I do know is that after our first night, our sex life could only be described as fabulous. Incredible! We'd enjoyed each other's company completely while we were courting, but fell deeply in love as our time together progressed. I'd certainly been intimate with a number of young women before Grace Goddard and my mother cooked up the marriage between Norma Jeane and me, but never in my wildest imaginings had I known a girl who so utterly enjoyed having sex. Our lovemaking was complete joy, abandonment, surrender and pleasure. We laughed and played at sex, rolled around like squirming puppies and could never, ever seem to get enough. We loved without embarrassment. There was nothing we wouldn't try, no room we wouldn't try it in. I'd had no idea when we married that we would be able to satisfy each other so happily. Our sexual times together were just quite simply wonderful. I'll never forget them. I know Norma Jeane enjoyed our sexual play, and she was not shy about asking me to join her at every opportunity and by join I do mean join!

How well I recall one day--a broad daylight sort of day when we were driving through a built-up and heavily populated section of the San Fernando Valley. She reached over and squeezed my hand. Now any other guy would have interpreted that move as an expression of affection from his lady, and would have smiled, squeezed her hand back and kept on driving. But I knew better. Norma Jeane wanted to make love. Right now. Right there!

Whenever this happened, I'd always say, "But honey! We've got a nice private home, and a beautiful bed!" and she'd slide over and lean against me and say, "Oh Jimmie, it's so much more romantic right here," and so we'd park and do it. Every tingle time. She didn't have to convince me!

This time in the San Fernando Valley when the impulse hit her, she squeezed my hand.

"Pull off here!" she said, urgency in her voice. "Pull off here, Jimmie!"

"Norma Jeane," I said, looking at her beautiful, eager face.

"Somebody's going to see us. There are an awful lot of people around here!" but I pulled off anyway. I knew when this lady wanted to make love, nothing would stop her, and I was not exactly unwilling to oblige her.

"Besides," she said to me breathlessly, as we began to couple in that car on that street, "Who cares? We're married, aren't we?" I laughed. "By golly Norma Jeane, you're absolutely right! So what's the difference?!" and we got down to business. I think we probably still hold the record for being the only married couple who had sex on half the country roads and more than a few village streets of the San Fernando Valley, and it was always great, always joyful and carefree. Norma Jeane Dougherty and I made each other very happy sexually. And every way.

And, on a day to day basis, Norma Jeane also simply radiated sexuality. She didn't have to be making love to be sexy. She just had "it," and anyone meeting her knew what "it" was. But honestly, I don't know if she knew it. She was so young, so incredibly innocent, trusting of everyone. As we grew together, I wanted to protect her because of this trust she had in everyone. She was beautiful. She was special. (That's a word so overused today, but in her case, it applied. She was unique and every day I knew it more and more.)

In later years I'd read that Marilyn Monroe remarked that she wasn't often sexually satisfied with lovers. I can and must conclude that if this were so, those men were lacking in something, because before Norma Jeane became "her," she adored sex between us.

As our time passed together, I became keenly aware of the enormous appeal she had for other men. She never once gave me the slightest reason to worry or feel jealous. I was Norma Jeane's whole life, and we both knew that. But still, men just seemed to be drawn to her. They stared at her wherever we went, moved in closer. They wanted to touch her and speak with her. I knew that and soon developed an attitude with these guys, looking at them in a most threatening way, and that usually made them back off. I don't really know what she did when I wasn't around, but sometimes I think she wasn't aware. Other times---well, she sure was.

I recall one time when my buddy from work, a guy by the name of George Yager came over to invite me to go to the fights with him. I was unable to attend, but suggested to George that he take Norma Jeane, knowing how much she loved things with a lot of action in them. So he took her. I wasn't worried. I knew George well and trusted Norma Jeane utterly. She had a terrific time at the fights, and the next day, I got three phone calls from well-meaning friends, warning me that they'd seen my young wife out with another man. I surprised all of them by saying that it had been my idea.

But as time passed, I have to admit I was beginning to notice more often Norma Jeane's special effect on men. They were drawn to her like moths to a flame, and sometimes seemed physically unable to keep away from her. I noticed how men stared at her, seemingly unable to not. Women were affected by her also, but not nearly the way men were. Most of the time, it made me proud that I was the husband of this wondrous, glowing creature. Other times I was extremely uneasy. But my Norma Jeane never once gave me reason to doubt her faithfulness and love for me.

I think back sometimes to a day when I was in a small supermarket in Van Nuys. I hadn't shaved for three days or so and the owner wanted to know what I had on my face. (It occurs to me that this is a rather stupid question to ask a man who obviously has a growth of beard on his face. People never cease to amaze me.)

"I'm growing a beard," I said, as if it were any of his business.

"You idiot!" the guy explodes at me. "Whatchu doin' that for? With a beautiful doll like Norma Jeane as a wife, wadda you want to have a beard for? You'll wreck your looks with a beard. She shouldn't have to be married to a guy with a beard!" I shaved it off the minute I got home. Now I knew for certain. Norma Jeane Dougherty had a very strange and compelling influence over men, even men she—and I—hardly knew.

As another example, there was the time we met the great cowboy star, Roy Rogers. I used to buy my sporting gear at a western shop in Van Nuys and one day, Norma Jeane and I were in there together. Roy Rogers was checking out some new saddles and saw me. We had a slight acquaintance and nodded to each other.

And then he saw Norma Jeane. His entire demeanor changed. The famous Roy Rogers grin spread across his face and he tipped his hat at her. Obviously the sight of my gorgeous wife delighted him.

"Roy, this is my wife, Norma Jeane," I said.

"She's lovely," he said emphatically, grinning straight at her. He'd forgotten I was in the room! How sweet it was for me to see my dear wife glow at that compliment from the famous cowboy star. But she never let go of my arm and oh, how I loved that she clung to me the way she did, especially when she felt vulnerable or frightened. And especially when she was around handsome male movie stars! As I recall it now, on our way home, she never mentioned any special desire to be in any way connected with movie stars or be in the business.

Truly Norma Jeane had no awareness that she was beautiful, but oh, how she wanted to be. She would rinse her face sometimes fifteen times because she was so desirous of having a perfect complexion. She swam, was very athletic and ate plain, wholesome food. She even lifted weights with me, to keep her body in good shape, and back then, women didn't lift weights much. She hunted and fished with me.

Norma Jeane was beautiful and witty, and not dumb. Naive, but not inarticulate. When I look back, I wonder now if there was an ulterior motive to Norma Jeane's doing all of those physical things to keep herself looking as beautiful as she could, but I never saw that back then. And I don't think she was that complex, or devious. And of course, now I won't ever know, but in the end, really, it's not important. I was tormented for some time with questions of what was in her mind when we were first married. But it doesn't matter any longer. There is no point in anguishing about what is or was in another person's mind, or how it affects them, or how it affects the people close to them. I just refuse to waste time trying to figure it all out. Life is too short and too sweet and I have other things to think about.

But sometimes, when I'm out fishing alone on our beautiful lake in Maine, I begin to reminisce, to think back to that time fifty odd years ago, and I often remember the first time I met Norma Jeane at the Goddard's. She surely had womanly assets which I couldn't help but notice, even though she was so young. (Norma Jeane's physical development was apparent long before other girls her age.) These were her beautiful face and body, and her quick wit. Yes, she was a little naive sometimes--after all, she was still just a child. And when she used a word incorrectly, she was the first to correct it. She was so mature when we married, even though she was only sixteen, and she grew and matured enormously during our short marriage. When I look at the photos of us at our wedding and then a few years later when she'd begun modeling, I can see such a difference in her. Anyone could.

And Norma Jeane was so very critical of herself. Too critical. A perfectionist really. I'm no authority on such things, but perhaps this happens when a little girl grows into womanhood without too many friends along the way, without the security of strong family ties. Perhaps she wonders all the time if there is something wrong with her. Maybe she's always frightened because she sees that she's always left out of things. Possibly she thinks she's different from everyone else, and especially her peers. Maybe she becomes super-critical of herself, a perfectionist, a perpetual worrier about her looks and appearance so that she can not only measure up to the others, but can go beyond them. Maybe she thinks she's really ugly or she's really beautiful and if beautiful, then perhaps no one will love her for herself. Maybe this is what happened to my Norma Jeane. I'll never know what worries she had, or how much she may have anguished about these things. Not in this life, I won't.

I recall how the child in Norma Jeane would surface

unexpectedly. Norma Jeane had been deprived of so many childish pleasures, being bounced from foster home to orphanage and back and forth. So it was no surprise to me when that little kid she carried inside of her would suddenly come out. I understood and loved her when she became babyish, and also when she did a quick turn-around and became a mature, responsible woman. She was changeable and could amazingly switch roles in an instant. But I think, young as I was, I was wise enough back then to encourage Norma Jeane to be whatever she wished to be at the moment, to be free to be whomever she wanted or needed to be. I know I was understanding, that it was important for my young wife to keep in touch with that small child hidden in the precociously mature body of Norma Jeane Dougherty.

Look. I don't want to come across here as this wise old sage who knew everything and existed simply to "guide" this young and innocent child bride of mine toward a life of great depth and wisdom and maturity. That was hardly the case. If anything, it was she who taught me a great deal about life. No. It's just that I was older than Norma Jeane was, and there really is a lot of maturing that happens to a person between the ages of sixteen and twenty, and she was sixteen and I was twenty so you see, I really was "wiser" than she in many ways. I mean I'd been around more. She was still a little girl in a great many ways when we married.

That little girl inside of her came out again one Sunday when I left her in the living room on Archwood shooting craps with my brother Marion. I smiled at her. She looked so grown up sitting there playing that adult game "with the big kids" as I walked by her on my way to take a nap: (I was still on the graveyard shift and so sleep was important to me.) I ran my fingers through her thick, glossy hair and she grinned up at me. God I was happy to be married to her.

"I'm gonna sleep for a while, Norma Jeane," I said. "I'll see you later."

"See ya, Honey," she said, and went back to the game. I went into the bedroom, pulled off my trousers and shoes and fell into a deep sleep. But even in the deepness of that nap, the squeak of the door awakened me and in the darkened room I saw Norma Jeane sneaking over to my trousers, glancing over at me. I was about to speak, but decided not to, wanting to see what she was up to. Suddenly, I realized she was going through my pockets. I sat up.

"What are you doing, Norma Jeane?" I asked her, my voice sharp. She jumped and turned toward me, her hand buried in the pocket of my pants. I could see she was plainly mortified. Her face became crimson and her eyes filled with tears.

"Jimmie!" she said, her voice a gasp. "Oh, I thought you were asleep."

"Obviously."

She pulled her hand out of the pocket and stood still, looking at me. I knew she was ashamed. The tears welled and spilled down her cheeks and I knew she was about to cry hard.

"Norma Jeane, why do you need money in the middle of a Sunday afternoon?"

"It's my dolls, Jimmie, my darling dolls," she said, holding back sobs. "You know how important they are to me, that I love them. They've always been with me Jimmie. And now," her soft voice broke and she now sobbed in earnest. "Now your brother Marion has won all of them in the game. Every single one of my dolls. I have to borrow some of your money so I can win them back. But Jimmie—Jimmie—I—I just keep crapping out all the time." Tears now poured down her cheeks. Her lower lip pushed out and began to tremble.

I stood up and put my arms around her. "Oh darlin'," I said. "You'll never learn about us Doughertys, will you? Don't cry, Sweetheart. You're just being had. My brother Marion is about the biggest tease in all the world. I promise he doesn't want your dolls. Not in the least!" I began to pull my pants on. "Come on with me, honey," I said, my arm around her shoulders. "I'll get your dolls back for you. And for free!" And I did. My Norma Jeane couldn't have imagined her life without her stuffed friends and I would never have let them be take from her. Where did they go, her ragged, worn old friends? Who has them? I wish I knew where they were. I'd love to see that forlorn little collection again, to caress and hold and touch them as she had. If I could do that I'd feel close to her again, if just for a little while.

I love to think and talk about the grown up woman in Norma Jeane too, and that part of her seemed to thrive on being my wife. She so loved to keep our tiny home clean, to shop for food in the local grocery store and fill her time until I'd come home and we could get back into bed together. We quickly grew to love having sex as often as we could. We were both young and trim and when we undressed, we'd stare joyfully at each other's nude bodies, and then charge to bed. So eager we were to make love, we could hardly wait to lock ourselves together as one, and often did not wait to turn out the light. Our sex life was wonderful, beyond satisfying. We enjoyed each other, teased and laughed and played in bed for hours. If I took a shower and she opened the door, she'd look at me and we would begin again, in the shower, in our bed and everywhere it took our fancy. We thrilled each other and gave endlessly, again and again. So compatible and happy, I sometimes thought I'd explode with the sheer ecstasy of being Norma Jeane's husband. She gave me much. I took much and it was that way between us, giving and taking with joy and gratefulness and pleasure. And tenderness. Always with tenderness.

An unmerciful tease, my new wife was always inventing all sorts of ways to coax me into having sex with her; but she never had to, not really, not for long. I was always a willing participant. We both were. For example, I'd come home from Lockheed and open the door to find her dressed in two tiny red bandannas, and I would not be able to stop myself. Norma Jeane and I happily exhausted each other. Sex was a huge part of our marriage. Not the only, but one of the biggest.

And folks, that's as far as I'll go on this issue. I am asked and asked to do a "tell all" about Norma Jeane's and my sex life but I will not do that. I am told I "remain always the gentleman" when I'm asked those rather intrusive and rude questions by people interviewing me today, and so I shall be. Always. It is no one's business, no one's but Norma Jeane's and mine, and because I am a spiritual man, I believe strongly in an afterlife and I know absolutely that Norma Jeane is watching over me and is proud that I've kept that part of our very short time together private. All our own. And we are glad that it's stayed this way.

I will never forget one warm night. Normally, we'd fall asleep with her head on my arm. This night, we'd fallen asleep completely naked as we always did, our arms and legs corkscrewed tightly around each other, Norma Jeane's head against me, her curly, soft hair spilling across my chest. I was deep in a contented slumber--and then I felt her shaking me. Gently, softly. I opened my eyes and looked up at her. My beautiful wife was sitting up in our bed. She'd pulled the covers down to our waists and a bar of pale moonlight splashed across our bodies, bathing us in silver milk. I stared at her. She was a vision--an angel who appeared as if dropped from a strange, unknown part of heaven. I reached for her and thought my hand would go through her. She was gossamer in that moonlight, a shimmering sprite, a being I didn't know and yet knew utterly. My heart flopped in my chest.

"Look Jimmie. Isn't it beautiful?" her voice, filled with wonder, was whispered glass. "Oh Honey, look! It's a full moon."

CHAPTER 9

In her second life, where she was the glamorous, glittering Marilyn Monroe, Norma Jeane wasn't often seen in outdoor, rough clothing, but when she and I were together, she loved being outdoors and wearing things like that. Right from the start of our courting, she showed me her passion for the sky, and mountains, lakes, pines and meadows. She said she loved living in a home with me, but her home was just her shelter with windows to look out at the world. Her love of nature was so strong, even up to the very end of our four years of marriage.

Was it all an act? Was everything between us a performance on her part? If it was, then she was a better actress than she ever thought she was. Sometimes I think about that, wonder if she had been pretending all along.

But no. Norma Jeane, if nothing else, was sincere with me and honest with everyone. I trusted her completely. I couldn't have been fooled for so long. She couldn't have fooled everyone we knew. I guess when you look back at a painful occurrence in your life, your mind wanders and goes into dark places where it shouldn't go. But no. She wasn't pretending with me. I mean after all, she was only sixteen and even though she'd had a hard life with many disappointments and scares, she wasn't that sophisticated and mature to be able to pretend her passions.

Norma Jeane and I loved to go fishing together and she was a pretty good fisherwoman. She became pretty good at hunting too.

This, obviously, made me very happy because they were two avocations I really enjoyed and had become quite good at in my youth when I hunted and fished for my family's food during those long, difficult early years. I taught Norma Jeane to shoot, and she became very good at it, as long as the target was in fact a target and not an animal. Sometimes, we'd take our guns and we'd climb mountains and get lost in the woods together. That's what she thought, but she was never afraid because, really (and I don't mean to sound like some big woodsman hero), there are and were no woods where I'd ever get lost. I've always known how to get out of the woods. But while Norma Jeane loved the hunting part of hunting, she simply would never shoot anything living. She was too tenderhearted to do that. I think, however, in time, she would have eventually changed her mind on that issue because we had such a powerful love for each other and a constant need to please. I lived to please Norma Jeane. I know she felt exactly the same way toward me. And to those who would accuse me of living in a world of wishful thinking, of having this sort of hazy twenty-twenty hindsight, no, I'm not hoping my wife Norma Jeane wanted more than anything else to please me--I know she did.

I remember the time I taught her to skin a rabbit I'd shot. She made the most comical face of revulsion during the procedure, but she went through with it and I was proud of her. Norma Jeane often made me proud.

I knew how much Norma Jeane had loved all animals in her life. Terribly humane and softhearted when it came to all living things, she never wanted to harm them, although she was not a vegetarian. Maybe she related to scared, lonely things, the way animals are sometimes, the way she'd frequently been forced to feel before our marriage. And so I understood how she hated the hunting and killing part of our life together, but for me, hunting had become a way of life. As I've already explained, when I was a kid, hunting meant my family could eat. It was the only source of meat for our table. I made certain my kills were clean and quick, a practice I continue to this day. One shot only. Our family could not afford the luxury of buying boxes and boxes of bullets. We made our own, and believe me, no animal ever suffered because of me. Never.

Thus, Norma Jeane and I would eat what I'd killed. We really couldn't afford to eat out at the best restaurants except for very special occasions (like the Florentine Gardens where we'd had our wedding reception) or the Coconut Grove where I bought Norma Jeane her first white orchid.

But my young wife loved to fish, and was not at all revolted by it. She learned to bait a hook quickly and with ease, and it was worth more to me than I can say to see how excited she got when she'd catch a fish. What a sight that was! Norma Jeane had learned to row boats when she was a very young girl, so when we could, we'd go to Sherwood Lake in Ventura County. I'd row and then she'd take over and I'd fish, but after a while, Norma Jeane would get so interested in my fishing, she'd let the boat drift far from shore and I'd be unable to continue casting. We'd always bring home loads of fish for ourselves and anyone else we could give them to, and it was enough to last a long time. Like the memories.

And so our larder was filled with fish and meat and Norma Jeane was a very good cook, especially when she paid close attention to a cookbook. She eventually became an excellent cook, and very proficient in cooking game, and even though reporters and so called "chroniclers of her life" made a big thing out of it, Norma Jeane in fact really did like to cook peas and carrots together because she loved the combination of colors. Whenever I read that today (and I think the carrots and peas thing all began from interviews I've given over the years) it bothers me because it sort of makes her sound like a simpleton, a young woman cooking foods solely because they looked pretty and forgetting about the nutritional aspect of it all. But that is wrong. She was very concerned for our health, and cooked big, hearty healthy meals for us. And I won't forget that my wife Norma Jeane's venison and rabbit meals were delicious, wonderful. I was very blessed.

I will never forget the time she cooked a catfish and served it up to me after I'd come home from work. She'd done a great job, but the fish was raw in the center and really inedible. I did try to eat it, to pretend it was cooked through, but I just could not. Norma Jeane's reaction was funny and sad at the same time. She was extremely embarrassed and really acted as if she was about to run out of the house. I stood and held her and assured her that it was no big deal, no problem and that I loved her. We laughed, but my dear wife, my little girl wife had a really hard time with rejection, on any level. Even when it came to my being unable to eat raw catfish.

There were glorious days when Norma Jeane and I went exploring, hunting, fishing, and playing in the outdoors. I look back and I remember my boundless happiness and how I loved her. I remember Norma Jeane outside almost more than I remember her anywhere else--the sun just lit her, somehow, oddly, as if from within. She glowed. She was so healthy and was so at ease in the out of doors. Whenever we could do it, we'd dress in our oldest, most baggy clothes and head out for another outdoor adventure. It was where she belonged. I wish you could have seen here there. It's like that song that Robert Goulet sings—"If Ever I Should Leave You" where he sings that he could never leave his love in any of the seasons because of the way she looked in each of them. Norma Jeane took on a certain "look" in all the seasons when she was outside. Spring and fall were best for her—she just glowed in all those colors. But really there was never a time or location when she didn't look ethereal, beyond beautiful, even in scruffy old clothes. Sometimes Norma Jeane would wear one of my old shirts so her clothes would stay clean beneath, and I clearly recall in one of her first modeling photos where she wore one and held it up at the shoulders by her fingertips to indicate to the viewer how huge it was on her.

I still grin when I remember my Outraged Young Husband's reaction to seeing my young wife dressed to go out on a modeling job and realizing that she was wearing no underwear.

"Hey! Norma Jeane!" I said. She looked at me. "Yes?"

"You don't have any panties on!" Norma Jeane stood as tall as she could (which wasn't very!) and smoothed her skirt down with her hands. She looked up at me again, her gaze level and cool.

"That's right," she said. "I don't."

"Well," I blustered, "Well--why don't you?"

"Because Jimmie," she said, her voice steady, "in my opinion, it looks very crude for underwear to show through lady's dresses. It's vulgar."

"Vulgar?"

"Yes Jimmie," she said.

"But Norma Jeane, what if you -- I mean what if you get into the wrong position and you show everything?"

She looked at me, exasperated. "Jimmie," she said, in that cool, logical tone she could use, "then I just will not get into the wrong position."

And even though her beautiful, womanly body was completely covered by those old clothes of mine she frequently modeled in, she was still powerfully sexy looking. She had an air about her--no, that's not exactly how to describe it. Norma Jeane Dougherty had more like an aura. She's so often been described as having that "glow" thing—and she did. I know I've said this before, but it bears repeating—It was always as if Norma Jeane was somehow lit by candles from within--candles with a somewhat special energy, more than mere candlepower. In another age, she would have been called an enchantress. In another age, she would have been burned at the stake for this strange, compelling quality of hers. I could hardly keep my eyes off her. I didn't try.

CHAPTER 10

Everybody has heard Marilyn Monroe's singing. "Some Like It Hot," and "Gentlemen Prefer Blondes" are a couple of the films where her singing voice could be heard. By the time she'd become the huge star she had, she'd had a lot of singing coaches and she learned well.

But when she and I were together, we'd often sing together, and her voice then, right exactly on key, was an unadulterated, purer version of her professional voice. It was sweet and light, a cute kind of voice and very soft. She never sang with great volume, but you had to listen to it-- the way you have to stop and listen to a songbird, if you really want to hear the melody. I loved hearing her sing.

And I loved to sing myself. Still do! I guess if I could live my life again, I'd do it as a singer. Well, maybe an actor. OK, both. I sang a lot as a kid, and sang with a group when I was in the LAPD. I've been blessed with a deep, strong voice and if you'll forgive a little poetic, visual description, when Norma Jeane and I sang together, it was like soft, silky lace sliding across rough, dark leather. And until the day I die, I shall never forget how she sounded when she sang the beautiful "I'll Be With You in Apple Blossom Time," the famous Andrews Sisters World War II hit song. I always become emotional whenever I hear that song, and it's never really stopped being played. Norma Jeane also sang "When you Wish upon a Star," the song Jimminy Cricket sang from the Walt Disney animated film "Pinocchio." She sang that hauntingly, as if she really wanted to believe the words "...makes no difference who you are. Anything your heart desires will come to you." What did my Norma Jeane's heart desire back then? Why couldn't I know? Why didn't I see? Was there actually something to see or to know then? Did she know it herself? I'll always wonder about these things. Always.

Norma Jeane and I had a lot of friends back then, and when we invited them over, she would become kind of quiet, letting me keep the conversation going for the most part. It may be hard to believe, considering her future fame as an actress, but Norma Jeane was an introvert. And I definitely am not. Now I do not mean to suggest that she'd sit in our livingroom with our guests and not speak playing the role of "good little wifey" and just bringing in food and drinks. No, she spoke, but she was sort of shy and really seemed to like it when I started conversations and kept them going. She spoke, but it was always softly. Still, because she was so compelling, our friends listened to her and watched her as she spoke. When she spoke! How could they have known that in a very short time they'd be watching her up on that big screen, the way she herself had watched all the great stars when she was a child.

I remember one time when I was playing the guitar, and we began to sing together. I was pleased, knowing how shy she could be, and we sounded really good. When we finished, she said, "You know, I did a musical thing when I was in school one time. It was a song called---let me try to remember--oh yeah, I guess it was `Schoolhood Days' or something like that. Well, the words were kinda like—umm—OK, I remember--`when we were just kids and we'd kick off our shoes and go swimming.'" And Norma Jeane got up and did a tiny dance and kicked off her shoes and one went sailing toward my head and missed crashing into my ear by no more than an inch. It smashed against the wall directly behind me. Everyone became silent for an instant and then Norma Jeane bent nearly in half with her raucous laughter, the way she'd laughed that night when she made me race behind the car shouting at her to put on the brake.

My new wife began to draw closer to my family. Norma Jeane had a special respect and love for my oldest brother Tom, and went to him with problems if I couldn't be there. And she got closer to Mom as time passed, and in fact later on, she lived with my parents while I was in the Maritime

Service in the Pacific.

Norma Jeane would confide in my mother when she was lonely while I was away. And she became even closer to Aunt Ana, and I was allowed to be Aunt Ana's friend too. As a matter of fact, she was the one who knew long before I did that Norma Jeane was dead serious about becoming a model or being in the movies. I guess Ana thought it would not have been appropriate for her to tell me about these plans, but sometimes I wish she had. It might have changed things. I may have been able to adjust or to work with Norma Jeane and her plans. I will never know, of course, but sometimes I will think about this issue and wonder if I'd had any idea at all, if I'd known,...if...if.

But all of that would come later. I was an extraordinarily happy young man with a stunning new wife, a young woman who assured me that I made her happy, that I was giving her the stability and love she'd craved so as a child, and who always told me that finally, she was safe. It was luck and timing and all sorts of things over which we had no control that brought us together then, and whatever it was, I was grateful, I was elated. I was, as I've said before and always will, blessed.

CHAPTER 11

I doubt anyone in the entire civilized world has not seen the beautiful calendar portrait of Marilyn Monroe, nude, curled against a red satin background, one arm bent alongside her face as she looks seductively from behind it. She's been quoted as saying she had to do it because she didn't have enough money to get her car out of hock, and that all she had on "was the radio."

I was stunned the first time I saw it. There she was--my Norma Jeane, naked for every eye to see. It's hard to express my feelings as I stared at the photograph. But then, it wasn't for me to make any of those decisions for her, or to even discuss her choices. She had "morphed" by then. She was no longer Norma Jeane. That Norma Jeane was gone. Not dead, but gone from sight, although I've always known that she was buried down, way way down inside of Marilyn. I always have wondered if Marilyn ever went down there to that place she'd hidden Norma Jeane and tried to look after her.

When I saw that calendar picture, my memories flew back to our time together, Norma Jeane's and mine. I remembered how she admired the nude body--hers, mine. But for her to be nude in front of anyone else, back when we were together, was simply out of the question, shocking, impossible. She was an intensely private young woman, the intimate and personal things held tightly to her.

I stood there, looking at that photo and smiled as I remembered one Sunday morning when Norma Jeane and I were sleeping late in the Murphy bed she so delighted in. My brother Marion and his girlfriend arrived unexpectedly and I began to crawl out of bed--nude as usual. Norma Jeane and I never wore pajamas to bed. She grabbed for me.

"Jimmie," she whispered loudly.

"What, Norma Jeane?" I turned back to her. "What's the matter. I'm just gonna get up and..."

"Jimmie. Don't you dare get out of this bed. Get right back in here! They'll see you!" I remember laughing and hugging her.

"OK, Norma Jeane," I said to her. "I won't let them see me naked."

I looked again at that now famous nude calendar picture of my former wife and then knew that Norma Jeane had abandoned some of her values and principles, things that had been so inordinately important to her when we were together. I sighed, turned my head and walked away.

My brother Marion really loved Norma Jeane and enjoyed teasing her, doing it every chance he got. Norma Jeane was so unwaveringly naive and refused to believe that people could occasionally be bad, and she wouldn't believe it of Marion. (This was something she seemed to continue believing, even after she became the "other" one. I know her earnest faith in the goodness in all people helped to bring about her end.) But Marion could occasionally get to her.

He sneaked into our kitchen one night while we weren't paying attention, and removed all the labels from our canned goods. Norma Jeane found it to be very amusing--for a meal or two. And then the joke became "Guess what's coming for dinner?" each night. I remember when she opened a big can of what she'd hoped was canned tomatoes and it turned out to be apricots--not so good in spaghetti sauce.

"That Marion," she'd fume. She always said that when Marion tricked her. But she loved him. He was important to her--a brother she'd never had. "That Marion," she'd grump. "Someday I'm gonna get even with that Marion."

And then, someday came. He arrived at our place more than a little drunk a few weeks after the can label incident.

"What are you doing here, Marion?" I asked him. He sagged into a chair. The smell of booze on him was strong. "You know, you're drunk, Marion," I said. "I am?" he answered. "Oh. Well, yeah, I guess I am. But hey Jimmie, I'm gonna get married!"

"You are? To whom?" I asked him. Marion pointed at the door. "To my girl," he chortled. "She's outside waiting for me. An' I want you two to stand up for us," he said. I laughed.

"Now, Marion," I began. "Speaking about 'standing up,' you can't even do that yourself, so why should I..." I turned and looked over at Norma Jeane. She frowned and shook her head and then grinned at me. I knew what that expression meant. I could read her face easily. She was telling me to not interfere, to go along with Marion's plan.

"Well Marion," I said, "Fine. You're too drunk to know what you're doing, but what the hell. Let's get you married. I'd be honored to stand up for you. Now stand up!" He did and I grabbed him, and we staggered together to the door and out to the car.

And so the four of us drove to Yuma, Arizona., and found a Justice of the Peace. Norma Jeane and I stood up for the slowly sobering Marion and this strange, new girlfriend he had----now his wife. He hadn't sobered up quickly enough because he went through with the ceremony. But on the way back, Marion became very sober and began to apologize profusely to his new bride, begging her forgiveness, telling her he should never have done such a thing. When we got to our house, he walked up to the door with us.

"How could you?" he whispered, looking back at the car with his new wife waiting inside, a look of abject panic on his face.

"How could we what?" asked Norma Jeane, her eyes wide and innocent.

"Yeah, Marion," I said. "How could we what?"

"You know damned well," he hissed at us. "How could you drive me to Yuma to get married when anyone with half a brain could see I was too drunk to know what I was doing?"

"You were?" Norma Jeane and I chorused.

"Well brother," I said. "We felt like going on the trip, and frankly, we didn't care if you got married or not."

Norma Jeane giggled for the rest of the night. For her, it was a great lark and, she said, "I guess he'll stop playing practical jokes on us for a while," and he did. Marion was chagrined and had learned his lesson. For a while at least. After a very short period of time, Marion and his agreeable new wife got an annulment or a divorce and never saw each other again.

Norma Jeane had come to love my other brother Tom, too, and when I was away during the war, she used to play poker with him, have long talks, or come to him with a problem I would have solved for her had I been there. They drew very close and became quite good friends. Years later when she'd become the great MM, Tom ran into her unexpectedly and was clearly delighted to see her. They chatted pleasantly for a while, and when Tom innocently asked if he might visit with her again, Marilyn Monroe became immediately cold, backed away and said "How much is it going to cost me?" Tom had been cut deeply by that remark. It was undeserved, but by that time, Norma Jeane was gone, vanished into the Marilyn Monroe who was occupying her body and mind, and Marilyn Monroe was always wary of people she'd once known, wary of people who loved her. Suspicious of them, afraid they'd take something away from her. She was so wary. How sad for her. How sad for the people who just wanted to be her friends. How sad that she had become convinced that everyone was after Marilyn Monroe for something, and weren't just anxious to renew an old friendship. I wish she'd been able to understand that not everyone on earth is a gold digger. I would have loved to remain friends with her, but it was not to be. I didn't fit.

CHAPTER 12

I was about to be drafted. It was late in 1943, and I'd been worried nearly constantly that it would happen. And then, in contrast, I'd sometimes worry about my not going into the service, considering every other male seemed to be going. I'd had a temporary deferment as "head of the household," but the war was escalating, and everyone was needed. I was becoming very aware that the military, the army in particularly, was breathing down my neck.

And to be completely honest, along with my feelings that maybe it was time for me to contribute to the war effort, I was beginning to have feelings of discontent at the Lockheed aircraft factory. Now please, read this the way I'm writing it because I know in this age of exaggerated political correctness, this might be misinterpreted. But here's what was happening; women were being moved in to Lockheed as helpers. So many men were off at the war in Europe and Japan and, it seemed, everywhere else. And so women were taking over their jobs. They had families and mortgages and desperately needed the income now that their husbands were gone. The work had to be done, and hiring women was a logical conclusion to a growing problem.

And at the risk of sounding patronizing, I will state here, on my honor, that they did a great job. They knew exactly what they were supposed to do, and they did it absolutely, no questions asked. They were wonderful, hard, committed workers. (Better than a lot of the men I worked with and that is for certain.)

But here's the problem; the women just did not have the brute strength for the jobs at hand. And back then, at my job, it required that sort of masculine brute strength to torque and tighten the clamps on the set-ups they handed over to me. There were no industrial robots back then, don't forget and a lot of the tightening work had to be done by humans. Male humans. Because these women did not have the strength to tighten these things to the utmost capacity, the results could cause intensely hazardous conditions. Men in the sky could have died if the machinery of their airplanes didn't work properly. People on the ground could have died because of airplane malfunction. It was an awful problem and it worried me constantly.

Because of that and other circumstances, because I was thinking so much about joining the military, I had to admit that I was no longer happy at work.

I regret now having done what came next, but without saying anything to Norma Jeane I began the process of enlisting in the navy. When I came home and told her what I'd done, she became nearly hysterical. I don't think I'd ever seen her as upset.

"Oh Honey," she wept, "your job at Lockheed is so important. Please Jimmie, please don't do this." She clung to me and cried. And I understood then, with her in my arms that way, begging me not to go, that she was again feeling abandoned, that if I left her, she perceived herself be alone again, with no one, even though my family would have cared for her. So I asked the navy to tear up my application papers and reluctantly, I went back to working at Lockheed.

But I could not shake the guilt. Nearly every guy I'd gone to school with was in the army or navy or some branch of military service for our country, and I wasn't. They were all at great risk, doing the fighting, being involved in the World War. It was hard back then, to not join up. The pressures were tremendous and frankly, I know I was being "looked at" by people we knew, and even those we didn't. I know they were thinking "you're a young, able-bodied young man with no children. Why aren't you over there?" Why wasn't I indeed? I had to do something. I had to take some sort of risks, too. I had to feel as if I was contributing something to the war effort, even if it meant protecting people on my own shores. And frankly, my manhood was at stake, also.

What could I do? I thought and thought and finally came

up with what I thought would be a decent compromise. I'd try to work in a place where lives were at stake, where I could make a difference and help people needing help. I went down to the local fire department and asked if there were any openings. There were and I filled out an application.

"You did what?" Norma Jeane screamed. She was angry. Shouting. "I thought that was all settled, Jimmie. You went and filled out an application without discussing it with me first?" She was shaking. "Jimmie, don't you realize that if you join that fire department, you'll lose your deferment?" I hadn't realized that. And so, my heart heavy, I went back to the fire department and asked them to tear that application up.

But it didn't make my guilt go away, my need to do something. So many young Americans were dying over there. I wanted to help stop that. I wanted to do something. And finally, I knew I was about to lose my deferment. I'd heard that if you joined the Maritime Service, you'd have frequent home leaves between trips. This seemed perfect. I could join, do my bit, leave Lockheed, and still, my Norma Jeane would see me fairly frequently. She would be reassured. She would understand that she was not being abandoned, that she would not be "out in the cold." Our marriage would continue. We'd be apart for only a few months at a time. A few months. A lifetime.

I remember that day when I finally went to join the Maritime Service. It was a brilliant fall morning. I remember each step of the way; I took the electric railway from Van Nuys to Wilmington and then the ferry across to Catalina where I was accepted as a sailor, or as a Merchant Marine.

I remember feeling absolutely terrible that day, for so many reasons, and of course, primarily because I'd have to leave Norma Jeane. I knew she was afraid. I knew she was harkening back to her childhood, feeling abandoned, seeing someone she loved walking away from her, wondering when she'd again have a stable, secure life with me.

I also felt terrible that day because the night before had

been awful, for both of us. The worst of my marriage--probably the worst of my entire life. I've never experienced anything like it. Norma Jeane had literally thrown herself at me. She clung to me and wept, her nails digging into my shoulders, my back. She was frightened and out of control.

"Norma Jeane, honey," I'd said. "Don't do this. Don't cry. I'll be home in a few months. They tell us that we aren't away from home nearly as much as soldiers and sailors are. I'll be back before you know I'm gone."

"No. Jimmie--you don't understand," she said, crying so hard she was losing her breath.

"What, Norma Jeane? Please darling, tell me." She was clutching me even more tightly then. So tightly I thought she'd never let me go. Oh God, I was tortured.

"Jimmie--oh Jimmie," she sobbed, "please, I'm begging you. Please get me pregnant. We've talked about this before, but now Jimmie--now--you've got to let me get pregnant now." The tears poured from her eyes and down into the collar of her shirt. I'd never seen her this upset.

"But honey," I began.

"No Jimmie--don't be reasonable with me this time. Jimmie, you're my love, my husband, all I have. If something should happen--if you should get killed then at least I'd still have a piece of you--a baby--our baby." She was frantic.

I pulled her down on the side of the bed, held her and rocked her. Her sobs continued. She was shaking, her face pressed into my shoulder. My Norma Jeane was desperately frightened. Now that she had me and a strong direction and focus to her life, she was terrified it would all end suddenly, and that once again, life would cheat her, abandon her, leave her out in the cold, lonely again.

"Norma Jeane, Sweetheart," I said gently, my mouth against her hair. "This is such a beautiful thing, a dear thought. But honey, let's wait 'til I get back, and I will be coming back to you, I promise. I just know I will, and we'll begin our family then. You know I want kids. I love kids. Having children with you is something I want more than anything in the world."

"Well then Jimmie, get me pregnant now. I can't stand to think that you could...you could..."

"Yes honey, I could die in this war. But I won't. And I don't want to leave you pregnant, Norma Jeane, because if I should be killed and you had a baby, and you're so very young yourself, you'd have to work to support the child. And what if you couldn't? I just can't bear the thought that our baby might end up as you did, in an orphanage somewhere, like you had to, my poor, dear darling. Please sweetheart, wait. We'll have babies. Lots of babies. I just don't think we should have one now, under circumstances like these."

But my wife didn't agree with me and she wept and cried and shook violently the entire night. I was left sleepless and raw---but I could not change my mind.

And so I was ashen the next day when I went to sign up with the Merchant Marines, now shaking so hard I could hardly hold a pencil. But amazingly, they found me in excellent physical condition, and signed me up. Finally I was going to serve my country. I was proud. And, I was very scared.

And oh, how I've anguished all these years about my decision regarding having children with Norma Jeane just at that point in our lives. Really, I thought it was the best decision at the time, and one I truly had given much thought to. Did I come across as arrogant with the woman I loved so dearly? Was I pretending to be wiser than my years? All grown up and the man of the family? Did I give her dreams and wishes enough consideration? Was I completely insensitive to her needs? Had I been too harsh? I think back and wonder if we'd had children and she'd become "Her," what would have become of our children with a mother named Marilyn Monroe? And then I ask myself if she'd ever have become Marilyn Monroe if I'd gotten her pregnant when she so desperately wanted it. Would she have suppressed her urges to be famous, loved by millions, a glittering, glamorous movie star if she'd had kids? And are suppressed urges such as those healthy for anyone? Would she have looked back over the years of being a mother and eventual grandmother and wished she'd at least have tried to be an actress? And would she have been bitter? Unfulfilled? Who can know these things? I didn't then, I can't now. The questions stay with me.

And, those questions sometimes would whirl around in my head, and sometimes I've wished I hadn't been so hardheaded on that issue, that I'd agreed to have had a child with her. I've always wondered what a child of Norma Jeane's and mine would be like, look like, and the thought still makes me ache.

And what gives me even more pain about this is that Norma Jeane did love children and instinctively knew how to care for them, and I knew that. My brother Marion had two children with his first wife, the one he married before his rash and regretful Yuma marriage, and he frequently brought these two young boys to our home to visit. Norma Jeane loved looking after them. She'd feed them, make sure their clothes were clean, that they took daily baths. She played endlessly with them, played like a child herself, sang to them, read them the funny papers. It was sheer joy to watch her with those kids and I'd think to myself "oh, what a wonderful mother she'll be one day," and I'd smile and be happy at the thought of it.

Marion's boys were utterly content when Norma Jeane was in the room with them. They loved her and she calmed them. Norma Jeane Dougherty would have been a wonderful, sweet mother to our children, had we had any. They would have been so lucky to have her. I grieved when I read over the years that she had miscarriages, because I knew how desperately she wanted a baby and somehow I could feel that pain from her although we were permanently out of each other's lives. It was to be denied her, and I know I was part of that denial. And I'm sorry I was. Forgive me Marilyn. Forgive me, Norma Jeane.

CHAPTER 13

And so I left. Norma Jeane was on the very edge of hysterics that day. It tore me to pieces, seeing her like that. I thank God I'd had the foresight to move her in with Mom while Dad was doing some construction somewhere else. If I hadn't known she'd be cared for and nurtured by my mother, I just know I could not have left Norma Jeane. I'd have been a deserter before I'd even begun! No, I could not have left my young wife alone. Absolutely not.

I watched my mother take her in her arms, hold and cuddle her, give her comfort. My sister Billie had come down to say goodbye too, and she held Norma Jeane's hand. Watching these three women, watching the two older ones giving such care and loving attention to Norma Jeane, I was soothed. I looked into my wife's reddened, tear-filled eyes and knew that she was completely secure--she knew without a single doubt that she had a family. But still, she was afraid.

And so I could leave. My heart was heavy, but I knew I'd left my beloved Norma Jeane in good, strong, loving hands. They would take care of her.

I'd be going through five weeks of basic training, and after a couple of days at the Maritime Training Base on Catalina, I was given permission to call home. Norma Jeane was utterly thrilled when she heard my voice. My eyes filled with tears when I heard her joy. It was as if I'd been gone for a year! It was so hard to hear her and not touch her, to not be able to hold her.

Many, many phone calls followed—long ones. It was like courting all over again. We desperately wanted to be with, and to touch each other. The longing in our conversations was strong. I used to think sometimes, hearing her words, her whispers, her bubbling, sweet laughter on the phone, that the ache in my heart to be with her again would split me into pieces. I thought I could not endure it. She told me she thought she also could not.

And then--a miracle! Maybe some would think it was a small one -- perhaps a fluke, but for us, it was as if we'd been handed a basket of diamonds! I discovered that I'd been made part of a ship's company on Catalina Island, where I would be staying as my very first permanent assignment.

I couldn't wait to get to a phone. "Hey Baby," I yelled, "I'm gonna bring you over here! We'll be together." Wow! Norma Jeane let out a shout of joy that nearly knocked the phone out of my hand.

"I'll find us a place to stay here. You're gonna live here on Catalina with me, Norma Jeane! Can you believe it?" But she didn't answer because she'd rocketed up to Cloud Nine. I had to hold the phone away from my ear because she was screaming and crying with such abandoned joy.

"We'll pick up right where we left off, darlin'," I laughed, but again, she couldn't possibly hear me.

And we did exactly that.

CHAPTER 14

I found an apartment for us in Avalon on the side of a hill. We packed up a few suitcases, a bunch of boxes, a pretty good sized dog on a leash and climbed aboard a ferryboat called the Avalon, which was a cruise ship available to ferry people back and forth from Long Beach.

But my dear wife got seasick on that short journey. We'd taken that trip before a few times, when we were first married, and she always gotten seasick, so this time was no surprise. I remember one time it was so bad I took her to the crew's quarters and had her lie down in an empty bunk. About five minutes later, a sailor came up to me while I stood at the rail.

"They tell me," he said, "that the dame in my bunk is your wife." Now, this kid had a bad tone to his voice. I didn't much care for it. I turned and looked squarely at him. He was behaving in a definitely uncivilized way and it just wasn't the right time for it. I drew a deep breath and stared hard at him.

"For your information," I said, "that lady is no dame, sailor, and you're right, she happens to be my wife. And also, she is sick." My voice was rising. Speaking normally I can blast the ears off a brass can, and this time I was speaking way beyond normally.

The sailor's voice rose too. "Well," he bellowed back, "She's not gonna mess up my bunk by gettin' sick all over it. You get her the hell outta there!"

One of the ship's officers heard all of this and came running up to us. Norma Jeane was moved to the deck where the fresh air revived her somewhat. It wasn't a big incident, but it could have become one. No one, absolutely no one ever had permission to refer to my precious wife as a "dame." And especially no punk kid with an attitude problem.

But life sometimes hands us a juicy morsel for just no reason, and as things turned out, that sailor, less than a year later, wound up as one of the rookies I had to train in the Merchant Marine boot camp. I can still remember his face when he saw that I was the one who'd be in charge. It didn't take much to see that he suddenly had a few very serious concerns. He was a sorry sailor for all of those five weeks. All of them.

Our little apartment looked straight across at the mansion built by one of the Wrigley's heirs. Sometimes, Norma Jeane and I would sit on the terrace of our apartment and gaze across at that huge, old home. We'd hold hands and dream and talk about owning a home like that one day, about how we'd fill it with our kids and spend the rest of our lives there together in happiness, in love. Wouldn't that have been something! Imagine, Norma Jeane coming from her strange, sad, lonely background and I from my poor childhood where I had to shoot the family dinners. What a change it would have been if we'd been able to get that mansion.

And my Norma Jeane never got one in her lifetime anyway, after she'd begun her new journey. She never became a wealthy woman. Marilyn Monroe gave all of her money away, or spent her earnings foolishly on clothing and cosmetics; Marilyn Monroe was willing to spend anything to keep herself looking young and beautiful for those cameras, for those mobs of adoring fans. Poor Norma Jeane. Poor, dear Marilyn Monroe.

And, of course, there was the endless therapy. Those sessions must have seriously drained her funds. The shrinks who got hold of her really had a meal ticket in Marilyn Monroe. I wonder sometimes if they just didn't allow her to get better, if they kept telling her she had to keep on coming back, over and over. Were their egos involved? Did they love that they were treating the world's most famous sex symbol? Marilyn Monroe had become so celebrated, they must have thought she was very rich.

I still have sweet memories of our time in Catalina. The island was, back then, still something of a resort. The homes dotted about were soft pastels. Everywhere we looked we saw softly colored beauty. The flowers and water, the homes, the way people dressed. Catalina was for us a Paradise. We were young and in love and we were very happy.

Even though our tiny apartment came furnished, Norma Jeane added small touches to make it look more gracious. I remember all the plants she bought and cared for. I remember that she'd put most of her doll collection away. My Norma Jeane was growing up. She was nearly eighteen, after all!

I did my part of adding to the home decor also. I brought in one of my old hunting trophies, a bear head that still had some fur left on it. We put it on the floor like a bearskin rug and one night, I got up in the dark to go to the bathroom and stubbed my toe on that old bear's mouth and cut it pretty badly. And just as she'd always do in situations where I looked like a dope, she began to laugh wildly! My young wife had an incredible sense of humor and if anything funny happened, you could always count on her having a good, hearty, belly-laugh over it.

Sometimes when I'd watch my dear wife as she laughed so hard at life's screw-ups, I'd wonder if her mother ever would laugh like that. I didn't see much of Gladys, but what I did see of her, there was never any display of humor or laughter or gaiety. Maybe Gladys had those things at one time in her life. She was a beautiful woman at least. I just never saw any happiness from the woman. Never a giggle, a loud laugh, a simple chuckle. She never told a joke or reacted to one. Nothing.

There was a club on Catalina called the Tuna Club and a huge outdoor park filled with every sort of exotic bird. I remember a crazy Myna bird in that bird park. He'd give out with this piercing wolf whistle and would then squawk "Are you a wise guy?" for some reason whenever a girl would walk by. We laughed at that nasty old bird.

There was white sand and a fabulous view that gave

Norma Jeane a sense of still being in normal civilization. Beyond the town was the harbor dotted with small craft, all in motion, moving in every direction like white seabirds paddling about, and way off in the horizon we could see Long Beach.

Sometimes in the evening, I'd go skin-diving for abalone and lobster and we'd call in some friends to join us for a fabulous feast on the beach. But mostly, it was important for us to just spend our evenings by ourselves. I'd often play the guitar and sing to Norma Jeane. She loved sentimental songs, and I remember one more than any other--"Tears on my Pillow."

Tears on my pillow each morning,

I cry when I dream about you.

When I should be sleeping, I just lie there weeping,

Wond'ring if you're weeping too.

Norma Jeane would laugh and tell me that I'd pronounced the word "pillow" so professionally. "You sure knew an awful lot of pillows in your day, didn't you Jimmie?" she'd kid me. She used to love to tease me about my "past" with the ladies--but she knew that now, there was no one else. How could there be? I knew I was married to someone so fabulous, so curiously unique. She enchanted me, my Norma Jeane did. She had the ability to do that, to enchant men, a lot more than she realized then. But she found out later.

It was a paradise back then for my beloved bride and me, and we explored the entire Catalina Island whenever we could. We knew our days together were numbered, that in time I'd be leaving, but we didn't speak of that or think of it. We ached when we thought about being separated and held each other, and so stayed close and lived and loved for the minutes we had left.

And we didn't have too many minutes left, but we didn't know that then. Did she? I wonder if something in her mind, her heart was telling her that something else was coming into her life. Something that would not include me.

The population of the island was mostly uniformed men

as the government began to monopolize it more and more. Norma Jeane was disturbed to discover that most of the women on the island were old ladies who had been allowed to remain in their homes as the area became more militarized. There were officer's wives there, living with their husbands in permanent companies like mine.

Norma Jeane didn't have an awful lot to do while I was away at work. She was always a perfect housekeeper and I was never ashamed to bring anyone home. The place shone. She loved doing that, and I know that's not exactly politically correct to say today, but in fact Norma Jeane took great pride in keeping a shining clean home. I've read that she was the same when she was married to Joe Dimaggio and Arthur Miller. And her cooking skills improved constantly.

But after her housework was done, Norma Jeane would spend part of every afternoon grooming herself for my arrival home in the evening. I was lucky enough to have been assigned a job as a physical instructor for the new recruits. But coming home in the evening was like--well, it's hard to say this without sounding silly, but she made it such a special time the way Christmas, Easter, and Valentine's Day are. I knew every night when I opened that door, that this young goddess would be waiting for me, looking perfect, waiting to make us happy, to please both of us.

Norma Jeane loved to wear white. She would wear pure white dresses, or white slacks or shorts with a white blouse. She kept these clothes in immaculate condition. She had the cleanest sort of beauty. It's so hard to explain, but the "glow" people speak about when they try to describe Marilyn Monroe, really existed. Honestly, she could just turn it on somehow. I've read how she could "be Marilyn," or she could chose to not be, how over the years she could walk down the street of a very busy big city without being recognized at all and she'd turn to her friends and say "You want to see me become `her?' Watch this." And Marilyn would quite suddenly become "La Marilyn." She'd change before their eyes--her attitude, her aura, her walk, her sexuality--it would all begin to ooze from her, and people would stop still and stare, immediately recognizing her.

But for me, she was always just Norma Jeane, my shining wife. Sometimes when she'd be all in brilliant white, she'd put a brightly colored ribbon in her thick, curly, dark blonde hair and it would be a lovely, contrasting touch of color.

And then one day our friends gave us Muggsie, a collie. She had a long brown, white and golden coat, and Norma Jeane kept her just as fresh-scrubbed as she kept herself, bathing that long-suffering dog nearly every single day.

How well I remember Norma Jeane putting on a pair of white shorts and a white halter-top and walking to the commissary for our groceries. She turned a lot of heads back then and I was always so full of pride for her. She was Norma Jeane Dougherty, my wife. I never worried when she looked like that in public. I never asked her to "tone it down." I've always been blessed with enough of a sense of self that I would not become jealous or threatened when I saw how men stared at my wife. I think my being centered gave Norma Jeane a feeling of security and confidence. She knew she could count on me. She understood absolutely that I would never disappoint her, or abandon her, or let her down in any way. She could depend on that. I thought I could depend on her, too.

However, I'd begun to notice mood swings with my wife. Dark moods. Fears. Sometimes she'd withdraw into herself, but when she saw my concern, with an obvious great effort, she'd pull herself out. I remember feeling uneasy, worried, but I'd put it all away when she came grinning at me.

I loved watching her with Muggsie. Norma Jeane would play with her constantly, and speak to her, touch and stroke her all the time. That dog adored Norma Jeane too, and was at her side constantly. I understood that Muggsie was a substitute for the baby Norma Jeane wanted so very badly and I'd feel guilty about that, and it would pain my heart to see her so devoted to the animal, but I stuck with my decision. I knew if I were killed in the war, my child bride would have a difficult time raising a child alone, and I couldn't bear to think a child of mine would end up being bounced around orphanages or foster homes for all of its life, suffering fears and lonelinesses.

And Norma Jeane had a mysterious side to her, something always there, but not, always invisible, but not, like smoke, here and gone. She was given to sudden inexplicably weird moods that were vaguely frightening to me, although they were mercifully brief. I've read that she was always afraid when she was Marilyn. They said she was often paralyzed with fear, and no one knew why. That she trembled and shook uncontrollably. That she could never show up on time for anything. Norma Jeane spent her years away from me with terror and demons. Was she frightened of being abandoned again? I wonder if she left me so that I would not leave her. I wonder if down in the depths of her soul where she kept her most private secrets hidden in the darkness, if she lived in constant terror.

And so, finally, I know and can accept that I made the right decision. If we'd had a child together and she'd gone off to become "her," our child might have suffered a lot. Oh Norma Jeane, I could have saved you. I could have. I so wish I'd been able to. I would have.

I remember Norma Jeane's menstrual periods being awful, terrible sessions, and those were times when I could never help her. She suffered horribly, and sometimes I thought she'd just pass out from the pain. Eventually, I convinced her to let me take her to a gynecologist who said the dreadful pains would probably disappear after she gave birth to her first child. I'll always remember her face when she told me that, the softly pleading look. It shook me considerably, since I'd talked her out of having a child. When she'd be knocked down by those killer pains, I'd wonder if she was blaming me, thinking that if I only agreed to having a baby with her, she would not have to suffer as she did. How could she have not?

In later years it was discovered that she had a condition called endometriosis which she might have been able to be cured of through surgery. She did suffer.

But finally, after all these years, I am at peace with the

decision I made which has tormented me so over the years. Yes. Finally. Or am I deluding myself? Am I trying to talk myself into thinking I'd done the best thing when in fact I don't really know that? I don't really know that at all. Maybe Norma Jeane had been right. Maybe I had. I'll never know.

But at least, thank heaven, the episodes of those horrendous periods were only a few days a month, and the rest of our time together was just sensational. Norma Jeane was dear enough to try to once make a joke out of her menstrual difficulties by sighing sadly when we were finally in bed together after one of my first trips to sea. She made me believe she was having her period, especially since she was wearing a sanitary napkin. I did a little mental math. It definitely was the wrong time of the month.

"Oh Norma! Come on!" I said and she burst into laughter, the sound so high pitched and sweet. She was filled with mirth and thought she'd played the funniest joke in the world on me. I always fell more in love with her at those times.

There is another thing that should be known about Norma Jeane back then. She was generous and kind. I've read that she always was this way as she grew older, and this was one of the reasons she never had any money. She gave things to people, including parts of her movie income. Of course as her life progressed, she stayed in debt a lot to keep her in clothes and make-up, and eventually, pills and booze.

But when we were together, whenever she had extra money, she'd always buy me a gift. Not a useless trinket, but something in good taste and often expensive. For example, she and I both admired General Douglas MacArthur. (This was long before his "disgrace" with President Harry S Truman.) Norma Jeane thought he was one of the world's great men, just a notch or two below Franklin Roosevelt, Abraham Lincoln and Mahatma Gandhi.

And so she bought me a bust of MacArthur and put it in a prominent place in our little apartment. Shortly after that, I bagged a pheasant on a hunting trip on the mainland and she thought the tail feathers were so beautiful, she placed them in a small vase next to the MacArthur bust. She was always doing things like that. She kept our home so beautiful with those little touches. She kept it so clean and appealing. Norma Jeane enjoyed the beauty of that pheasant, and I remember how she enjoyed cooking it. It was the first time in our marriage that we had pheasant and it was like heaven for us to keep cutting those rich, delicious steaks off that breast for two days or more.

I learned that Marilyn Monroe was a pretty fair drinker, especially toward the end of her life. I know she took a lot of pills to wake her up, to make her sleep. I guess her demons were much more painful and obvious to her as she grew older. She couldn't keep them at bay so easily, and alcohol and pills made them sink back into the darkness, at least temporarily.

But when we were together, when she was Norma Jeane, her choice of party beverage was ginger ale or root beer. One night my brother Marion, who'd never outgrown his love of teasing Norma Jeane, came over one Saturday with a full-unopened bottle of whiskey. He handed it to her and she looked at it and put it down on the table. We sat silently looking at it until Marion said "Hey, Norma Jeane. How's about your mixing us some drinks, OK?"

"Well sure, Marion," she said and smiled. She took the bottle into the kitchen and we cold hear her struggling to open it. She then came back out with three glasses, filled to the brim with the whiskey. She'd emptied the bottle. Norma Jeane put the glasses proudly on the table and sat down.

My brother and I looked down at the full glasses and up at each other and began to roar with laughter.

"Norma Jeane," I said, "Honey. You don't serve or drink this stuff like it's a glass of water. You put just a little into the glass and then cut it--you know, put in a little water or soda in with it."

Norma Jeane laughed. "Well," she said, "imagine how you would have felt if you'd drunk that whole glass. Imagine how I'd have felt. I don't even drink this stuff!"

But even though she was hardly a party girl, Norma Jeane managed to make friends with other instructors' wives, and she made one very close friend who lived next door. Norma Jeane and this woman spent a lot of time together--today they'd call it "female bonding," I guess. I enjoyed seeing my wife with a good friend. She didn't have many girlfriends in highschool and I know the memory of that hurt her. When she spoke of those painful years, I suggested to her that the reason the girls snubbed her was probably because she was so beautiful and well developed, far more than they were at a far younger age.

"The girls were jealous of you, sweetheart," I said to her, holding her hands in mine. "It's quite simple, really. They were just plain jealous."

"Oh no Jimmie," she said, looking hard at me. "No. That couldn't possibly be the reason. Nobody would be that mean. And anyway, I wore the loosest sweaters and blouses to hide my figure, so no one could see my shape anyway." I grinned at this child, my wife. She never wanted to think ill of anyone.

"Oh Norma Jeane, you're so dear," I said to her, and I pulled her against me.

When Norma Jeane was very young, even before her teens, she was astonishingly beautiful, and she matured physically too early, causing her young school chums to os-tracize her. She yearned for close friends and had one or two, but she was to be denied this and longed all her life for close trusted friends. And when they did present them-selves to her in her adult years, she welcomed them pas-sionately and then stepped back, frightened they too would soon leave her and no longer be her friends. Some people, the ones who were savvy and perceptive enough and could see past her fright and defensiveness, would stick with her to the end, but she often made that a difficult and nearly im-possible task for them. It was frequently just too hard for them because they were unable to live up to her oddly high expectations, her constantly challenging their fidelity to her,

her perpetual fears of their leaving her, her crazy jealousies--they just simply gave up. Very few people could withstand Marilyn Monroe's helpless, hopeless dreams and expectations.

Because of her tenuous background, Norma Jeane had been a super sensitive kid. Things affected her deeply and continued to for the rest of her too-short life. She always bled easily, not in the true sense of the word, but emotionally. It wasn't hard to cause pain in Norma Jeane. In Marilyn Monroe. I read about her chronic lateness, her terrors, her being unable to cope with the simplest tasks, her inability to ever sleep during normal hours causing her to be completely unable to fulfill ordinary daytime activities. I saw glimmerings of these things when we were married. After we divorced, after she became Monroe, these problems grew to frightening proportions and as the world now knows, as I know and knew, she was ultimately unable to control them.

When I think of our time together on Catalina, I have a vision of flooding sunlight and azure sea, a place where Norma Jeane and I laughed and played together when we could. On weekends, we'd go skin-diving. (Well, I'd do the diving and Norma Jeane would sort of look down into the water for me.) She didn't like it when I disappeared. Norma Jeane was frightened of seeing things she loved disappear. But she did love to swim and we spent hours on the beach. She had a wonderful white, one piece bathing suit which, at first glance, one might think she'd grown out of because her beautiful breasts were barely covered by that swimsuit. She caused quite a stir when she strolled around the beach in that because the people there were not accustomed to seeing skimpy swim wear. But Norma Jeane was not in the least embarrassed or concerned. At least this was one thing she could finally be proud of, her beautiful body, and her jealous school chums could not hurt her any more.

I, however, had some small concern. The island was heavily populated by males, not only the Merchant Marines, but regular marines were everywhere, being trained for underwater warfare, the equivalent of our frogmen of today. And those men on the beach when my wife was there made no secret of the fact that they were full of admiration for her. I would marvel at how she'd "turn on" when she was walking and knew men were looking at her. She'd do "the walk" seen later by millions in her films, but back then, she was just learning to do it, and she was very, very good at it! My Norma Jeane was in training for the lens of a camera back then, but there was no way I could know that. I wonder sometimes. I wonder.

Norma Jeane used to work out with one of the other instructors. His name was Howard Corrington, a former Olympic weight lifting champion. Corrington taught Norma Jeane how to lift weights as a way to improve her posture and her figure, (as if it needed improving.) Norma Jeane became surprisingly strong in her hands and arms, and occasionally, when we could, she and I would work out together. Remember, this was back when it was really unheard of for women to work out with weights or even to be very involved with physical fitness. But she was. Norma Jeane loved to take care of herself. She worked hard at keeping trim and in good heath. On other occasions, we'd go horseback riding. I remember one harrowing time when I could be a hero to my wife. It was a beautiful day and we decided to rent a couple of horses and ride to a point where we could see the ocean on the opposite side of Catalina Island. The trail was narrow--no more than ten feet wide, and there was a sheer drop-off on one side. I rode ahead. the horses walked slowly and we were drowsy in the brilliant sunshine. Turning my head, I could speak to Norma Jeane, and she'd answer lazily. It was a sun-drenched, wonderful day.

Suddenly, I heard her scream, a thin, high sound of fright sound. I quickly turned in my saddle and saw Norma Jeane's horse bucking for no discernible reason. My heart stopped and my skin turned to ice. I jerked my horse's head around and galloped back to my wife, grabbing the reins of her horse, and pulling it away from the edge. Norma Jeane was clinging to her horse for her dear life, her face chalky with terror. She was extremely terrified. Her face was contorted from the fear and she was fighting tears.

I dismounted and helped her off her horse and held her tightly. I could feel Norma Jeane's heart pounding against me.

"It's OK, honey. Just stand here and breathe deeply. Look out over the view. It's so beautiful, Norma Jeane--seeing a view like this with you here makes it more beautiful than it was meant to be."

"Jimmie, I'm..."

"I know, babe, I know. Look, you take my horse and I'll take yours. Yours got a little spooked, that's all. I'll handle him. Mine's a pussycat. Come on honey--you know what they say about riding. You've got to..."

Norma Jeane managed a small smile. "Thanks, Jimmie. You're my hero, you know. You always will be." She got on my horse and we continued the ride, and I was surprised that this terrifying incident did not make her afraid of horses or horseback riding because we had many more wonderful rides together in the sunshine of Catalina Island.

Norma Jeane and I never had a real honeymoon and I'm sorry about that. But there wasn't enough money then, or really ever in our short marriage. It was all I could do to manage taking everyone to the Florentine Gardens in Hollywood for our wedding party, but I would have gone into debt to do that. (And as I look back, I think I did!) At least I was able to give her that.

When I look back at that golden year we spent on Catalina Island, I think of it as the honeymoon we could never have had when we were first married. I remember joy and laughter and so much love it was dizzying. I keep saying I'm over her and that I've moved on. I am and I have—but when you have an experience like this, you really never forget it. If you're smart, you tuck it away in the secret place in your heart, a secret place like a small, beautiful box, a box no one can open but you, and you only go there to open it and let that secret out once in a great while, probably when you're alone and thinking about beautiful things from long past.

Happily, I only had to sleep away from my Norma Jeane's side when I had to act as master-at-arms in one of the barracks where the trainees slept.

I still grin when I remember coming home after one of those nights and knocking on my front door (I always had respect for Norma Jeane's privacy and never unlocked the door and surprised her.) I heard her voice inside. She called out loudly, "Who is it? Bob?" I stepped back and stared at the door. My mouth opened.

"What?" I called through the door. And I began to feel -- well, I was angry! Who the hell was Bob?

"No!" I yelled.

"Joe?" she called out. "No!" I yelled again, a lot louder this time. I could hear Norma Jeane coming to the door.

"Well then," she purred in her sexiest voice. "Is it Art? Jack?"

"Damn you!" I bellowed, really angry this time. I looked around, imagining hordes of the sex-starved marines and sailors coming toward me, all crowded on this small island with us and with very few women to help them through these difficult months.

I turned back to the door and hammered it with my fist.

"This is your husband. Jim! Now open the door and let me in!" I shouted. And she opened it, nearly doubled in half laughing her gutsy laugh. She'd planned doing this for weeks and enjoyed it completely. I'd reacted just as she'd hoped.

Those were sweet memories. They still are.

CHAPTER 15

I sometimes think about Norma Jeane's mother, Gladys. Norma Jeane didn't talk about her a whole lot and when she did, her voice got soft and small and there was hurt there. Gladys had put her baby daughter into the foster care of the Bolender's because she knew it was the best thing for the child at the time, but she'd always promised to come and get her when she had enough money and a home to keep her in.

And in truth, Gladys truly meant to keep those promises, and she hadn't utterly abandoned her child. She came for a visit every weekend when she could and spent what I guess today would be called "quality time" with her child.

But imagine what went through the little girl's mind on those weekends. She must have dreaded Sundays, when her beautiful, strange mother would leave her once again, and she must have been tormented by the notion that perhaps she wouldn't come back anymore.

Norma Jeane was not abused by the Bolenders. They were good to her, but very strict with this bright, golden child. Norma Jeane yearned to go home with her mother, but it was not to happen until much later and then, it did not work out very well.

Thus, because of my knowledge of this shaky ground my young wife had lived on in her early life (I suppose for her it was like living on very thin ice and wondering when it would break beneath her, pulling her under and leaving her in a dark, cold place forever), I understood her instant terrors whenever I disappeared for any period of time. I understood these strange interludes, understood these sudden sad, shadowy moods. She'd been bounced around like a useless, unimportant rubber ball for sixteen years until we married, and had tried to find happiness and security where she could. But often, she couldn't.

But amazingly, even with this tenuous background, Norma Jeane had a remarkable sense of humor. As I've stated before, I never saw that quality in her mother Gladys. I don't recall seeing Gladys even smile much, if ever. Perhaps at one time she did have joy, a sense of fun, before she succumbed to the demons chasing her.

Norma Jeane, the bone of her bones, flesh of her flesh, was able to see humor in everything, even if there wasn't much, and she loved to laugh. You could always count on Norma Jeane's being the first to laugh loudly and long at situations she perceived to be funny. I loved that quality in her. I was and am blessed with a rich funnybone and I have always loved a good belly laugh, so when Norma Jeane "let 'er rip" with her boisterous laughter, I was helpless against joining in, and we'd frequently collapse weakly together.

Humor, of course, is attractive to people and can act as a magnet, and Norma Jeane sought the approval of just about everyone. She desperately wanted to be liked for herself, not for her pretty face or amazing body, although she learned how to use those things to accumulate friends, and eventually lovers. I guess she yearned so desperately to be liked because love had been sort of parceled out to her when she was little, sometimes in pretty small increments. But, there was never enough. Sometimes now I think it must have been like a hungry person being given just an occasional morsel of food--he or she is always left wanting more and more to fill up the emptiness.

Perhaps, I do not know this for certain, but perhaps after Norma Jeane left me and was out on her own and did not have my very strong shoulder to lean on, she went hungrily after the love of fans, audiences, the whole damned world. And she got it and amazingly, still has it, decades after her death. What a weird phenomenon! Her picture is everywhere. But I suspect that eventually she discovered to her great trepidation that this global adoration was a terribly feeble substitute for the real thing. Norma Jeane was not easily fooled for long--not even by herself.

But she had one thing about her which drove me emphatically nuts, a habit she became extremely famous for in her professional life. Norma Jeane was impossibly late for absolutely everything. When I smartened up to this, I'd always tell her we were due someplace an hour ahead of the time we were actually supposed to arrive. That ploy worked a little, but not much. She managed to still be late.

I remember one Saturday in Catalina. There was going to be a block dance and the famous Stan Kenton's band was coming over to play. Norma Jeane got very excited about this. She poured herself into a really tight white dress and then began the Ritual of the Hair. That woman could literally take hours over her hair and this time was no exception. She fussed and fussed over it while I did a slow burn.

It started when we got married, this long, drawn-out getting ready procedure. It was not only the Ritual of the Hair, it was of the Bathing and the Dressing and the Applying of Make-up. These ceremonies could take forever. I never got used to them, never could understand why these procedures had to be repeated over and over, why the make-up thing could not be done once, why it had to be removed and redone too many times to count.

They say that when she was on the movie set, those rituals went on so constantly, Marilyn Monroe drove people nearly mad. Directors, actors--no one wanted to work with her. She cost film companies countless thousands of dollars every day, because she showed up so late. Seven, eight, ten hours late. Sometimes even days late. Time didn't seem to mean the same to her that it means to the rest of the world. I used to tell her that time, for her, was like a big rubber band. I've read how Marilyn Monroe would show up late on the set all the time. Or, she would not show up at all. Sometimes Marilyn would make an excuse, saying she was ill. Mostly, toward the end, she just never bothered to arrive. She was quoted as saying that "I am invariably late for appointments--sometimes as much as two hours. I've tried to change my ways, but the things that make me late are too strong, and too pleasing."

I do believe she said that. I believe she genuinely felt that way. She was never happy with her looks, always struggled to be better, consistently afraid she'd be rejected. I remember my anger at her for taking so damned long to get ready to go out. Today, the anger has turned to sadness at the memory of my beloved Norma Jeane taking so, so long to get ready for social events, so afraid that if she didn't look wonderful, no one would love her. Perhaps a more sensitive kid than most, she so desperately wanted to be liked and loved because she'd been allotted only so much love when she was a kid. Never enough. Like all little kids, she needed a lot of love but in all of those foster homes, the amount she needed to fill and satisfy her was denied her.

This may be ego talking, maybe just my imagination working overtime, and maybe these words come from a need I have, but I think that after Norma Jeane got out on her own and no longer had my shoulder to lean on, or my arms around her, she began to crave love from fans, more and more fans--and eventually from the whole damned world. Personally I think that's a pretty weak replacement for the love she and I shared, for real love itself, and from all I read about Marilyn Monroe during her life and after she died, I think she found that out. Norma Jeane was never easily fooled. She could always see the difference between real and phony, between the genuine and transitory. Oh, Norma Jeane. My poor, darling Norma Jeane. I would have saved you, Norma Jeane, if you'd let me, if you'd asked.

But anyway, I've digressed. Back to the block dance. This time, for the block dance, we were only a little late. I was amazed because Norma Jeane had begun very early in the day to prepare. She'd spent hours deciding what to wear, throwing clothing all over the room as she tried on an endless variety of outfits with the right shoes, purse, hairdo, stockings. She'd spent just as long bathing herself. I mean, how long does it take to get perfectly clean? Each move, each portion of this procedure was a painful ordeal for me although I tried hard to adjust and to understand. I've always been the sort of person who, long before I'm supposed to be at a destination, anticipates any possible problem I might encounter before the appointed time, or en route, so that I'm there exactly on time. I am annoyingly punctual and I guess I expect everyone to be that way, too. Later, when I became a member of the Los Angeles Police Department, I realized that we'd be forgiven if we never wrote a ticket, if we never made an arrest; but never would anyone be forgiven for being late. At roll call. In court. On your beat. Always on time. I was usually early, so you can see that Norma Jeane's lateness could be insufferable to me. She never realized how long a minute was--and time to her was truly like a rubber band.

"You know, Norma Jeane," I'd say to her, "you'll keep people waiting for your own funeral." I used to say that. Now I wish I hadn't. I didn't go to Norma Jeane's funeral but it turned out I was right.

Finally, that Saturday afternoon, we got to the block dance, her in that skin tight white dress, and we began to swing together to a tune called "The Peanut Vendor." We were dancing happily and within seconds I felt a tap on my shoulder. It was a young, eager marine cutting in. Being a gentleman, I handed my wife over to him, and I never saw her again for over an hour except for glimpses of her whirling by--each time with another man. Did I mind? No. Truly I did not. She was so radiantly happy, dancing like that with those guys. I was thrilled to see that. We'd both come from tough childhoods and to be happy was a goal. Our friends and acquaintances were envious of our happiness, and they often told us so. And that afternoon, watching my dear wife in the arms of so many men, every one of them different, all constantly cutting in on each other, she spinning and twirling about in that bright light, I knew how happy and thrilled she was and it gave me great pleasure. She was the belle of the ball and she was loving every second of it. And so was I. I was so proud of her!

The hours passed and eventually, I began to not love it so much. I began to feel a little uneasy and then, well, maybe a little jealous. I was beginning to feel shaken, standing there leaning against a building. And finally, my joy at her joy began to erode and I didn't much care for this scene. I found her and said "Let's go home."

Norma Jeane stopped dancing with whomever she was with at the moment and stared at me.

"If you don't mind," she said in a hard-edged voice, "I'd just as soon stay here. I'm having a good time."

There was harsh tension in the air between us. I kept my "steam" in control, but it wasn't getting easier. I stared back at her.

"Norma Jeane," I said in measured tones, "I think you ought to come home now because I've got to go to work in the morning and we've got to get some rest."

We looked at each other. I could see the resentment on her face, but I think she realized we were about to get into the first argument we'd had in fourteen months of marriage. And so reluctantly, her head down with embarrassment and anger, she left the party. I glanced at the soldiers and sailors watching and could see the envy on their faces. I did not feel any "pride of possession" then. Right then, I had the discomforting and vague feeling of being threatened. Right then, I'd begun to see that this glorious child-woman I'd married, loved men. And it was clear they definitely loved her back.

Now that I'm older and wiser, I see that I probably made a big mistake in forcing her to leave a party where she was having the time of her life just because of my needs, the demands of the breadwinner and all that stuff which would be called sexist today. After all, why did she have to leave the fun just because I had a job to go to? She didn't. She could have slept all the next day. Ah, but we're always wiser when we're older. All I could do at that point was to react to my own feelings, and my feelings were ones of discomfort and concern. And yes, jealousy. I was made keenly aware, that day, that members of the opposite sex had a strong chemistry, or pull, toward my wife. And I was tense because I began to suspect that she knew it.

And that day too, that block party, was the first time I

realized the enormous appeal this young girl had for a large group. It was phenomenal--unreal. She could control a crowd, please it, work it and make every member of it, even the women, fall in love with her.

Everything went right back to normal after the incident at the block dance, but I do recall other people connected with us being worried that I'd never be able to hold her. I know it worried my mother long before there was any concrete reason for it. Just a feeling, a strong sense in Mom. All I knew was that I adored this lady of mine more and more every day of our marriage. All I knew was that when I walked up the hill toward our home every evening she'd be waiting for me, in our home or on the corner.

There were other dances, and we went together, but I began to understand that there was no longer any point in complaining when she wore dresses that were just plain too tight. As I look back now, I realize that her shimmering, ever-present sexuality, the incredible attraction men had for her and she for them, was beginning to scrape at our marriage. I'd feel jealous, angry sometimes, but I stopped saying anything about it. I was beginning to clearly understand that I was married to someone who was different, on a different plane, -- perhaps on a different course. I was beginning to get a tiny glimmer that I'd married something slightly--well, unreal, illusory. A dream.

And I think now that these feelings I had on a daily basis may have been one of the reasons she never told me of her secret dreams to become a model or an actress, made her secretive about her plans for her future, fearful that I'd again make her "go home" the way I had at the block dance, because of my own personal anxieties. When Norma Jeane finally was discovered and embarked on a modeling career, it became like an outside affair, one of which I was cognizant and which I had to tolerate--even subsidize, because I loved her so much.

Gladys Baker and Norma Jeane Baker at 3 years old

Seventeen-year old Norma Jeane Dougherty photographed by husband, James E. Dougherty in Catalina California, 1943

Norma Jeane Dougherty at seventeen with Mrs. White and her baby in Catalina California, 1943.

Norma Jeane at seventeen in Catalina California, 1943.

Miss Ana Lower

requests the honour of your presence

at the marriage of her niece

Norma Jean Baker

to

Mr. James E. Dougherty

Friday, the nineteenth of June

nineteen hundred and forty-two

at 8:30 o'clock p. m.

at the home of

Mr. and Mrs. Chester Howell

432 South Bentley Avenue

Los Angeles, California

Reception

immediately after ceremony

432 South Bentley Avenue

Los Angeles, California

Mr. and Mrs. James E. Dougherty,
8:30 p.m., June 19, 1942.

Merchant Marine Seaman, J im Dougherty with his wife, Norma Jeane in Catalina, California, 1943.

Norma Jeane Dougherty photographed by the Old Lincoln Heights Jail in 1946
. © Joseph Jasgur

Norma Jeane at seventeen. Photograph by Joseph Jasgur, The Blue Book Modeling Agency, in Hollywood while Jim Dougherty was overseas in the Merchant Marine, 1944.

Seaman Jim Dougherty and wife Norma Jeane in Avalon California, 1945

Norma Jeane clowns for the photographer, Joseph Jasgur in 1945.   © 1945, Joseph Jasgur

© 1945, Joseph Jasgur

Norma Jeane Dougherty on Zuma Beach California, 1945
© 1945, Joseph Jasgur

© 1945, Joseph Jasgur

(above) Photographer Joseph Jasgur gave this
photograph to Jim Dougherty with the note, "Jimmie,
this is from Norma Jeane. She said she loves you."

(Right) Photograph taken by Norma Jean of Seaman
Jim Dougherty in Avalon, California, 1945.

Sunday December 3, 1944

Dearest Grace,

Thank you so much for the little black dress you sent to me, I just love it. All it will need is just shortening and taken in around the waist and hips. It was awfully sweet of you to send it to me.

As much as I like that black dress (with the pink satin) I just couldn't keep it, Grace becau

2

it just fits you and it looks so nice on you. I would have to have it fixed and besides I just wouldn't feel right about it, its such an expensive dress and all, though it was so sweet of you to want to give it to me. I shall just borrow it as I am doing with the hat.

I found out that its possible to buy a Gold Coast Monkey Coat. I shall write to you about it later.

I had very enjoyable trip from Chicago to Los Angeles, I wasn't sick even once. Everyone was just grand to me on the train, I'll ~~will~~ tell you all about it sometime.

Jimmie hasn't come home yet ~~but~~ maybe he might make it before Christmas, but he doesn't think so. I certainly hope he'll be home, it just won't seem right without him, I love him so very much, honestly ~~honest~~ I don't ~~too~~ think there is another man alive like him. He really is ~~awful~~ awfully sweet.

I hope your not working so hard now Grace, and ~~are~~ getting more rest and sleep. Please write to me about your self.

I shall send you more money a little later.

I can't ever tell you how much the trip did for me, I shall be ~~grateful~~ greatfull forever to you Grace. I love you and Daddy so much. I sure miss you Grace.

With Love,
xoxoxoyo Norma Jeane,
P.s. tell everyone at the studio hello".

James Edward Dougherty on left, P-3 Instructor, holding model 19-357 Smith and Wesson Revolver to advertise the Police Exhibition Pistol team.
Jim is wearing his Distinguished Expert shooting medal, the highest award given by the Los Angeles Police Department.

CHAPTER 16

And then, the idyll was over. Over more than I knew, back then. Maybe more than Norma Jeane knew. Ship's company kept cutting down on the permanent staff at the Catalina base, and shipping those eliminated overseas. As one of the last hired, I was on an early list for transfer to the western Pacific. It finally was final. I would have to go.

I wouldn't ship out for ten days, and at least during that time Norma Jeane and I would have to be busy. Being busy would mean we wouldn't really have much time to concentrate on the fact that we were separating, finally, the war would take me away, finally, she'd be alone and without me, finally.

But it was never really off our minds. We laughed and played and made love, but the ten days were narrowing down. We couldn't ever get the weight of that coming sadness away from us.

We began to shut down the apartment and that was sad. All of our mementos, our treasures--the things we'd purchased together, collected. We began to put our life into boxes.

Sometimes, while we worked together, we'd look up from our chores and stare at each other. And we'd smile and pretend that it didn't matter, but we knew it did.

"Oh, Jimmie," she'd sometimes say to me, in her whispery voice.

"Never mind, Darlin'," I'd say back to her. "Never mind." And we'd continue to pack the boxes. My family had moved to Hermitage Street in North Hollywood, and it's there Norma Jeane would stay until I got back from my tour of duty.

North Hollywood. How could I know then that the name of this place, this Hollywood, would figure forever in my life? That I'd be hooked into it, against my will, a place I would dislike, distrust and yes, come to resent.

Norma Jeane had always worked so diligently to keep an immaculate home for us, which made it wrenchingly sad for us to have to see our lovely, shining home reduced to the shambles that moving does to a place. All that was left were a few pieces of furniture.

She seemed distracted as she folded our curtains, carefully packed away our breakable treasures and packed our clothes in suitcases. I blamed the distraction on our imminent parting. Or, I thought, perhaps she was remembering all the times in her short life when she'd had to pack up her personal treasures and belongings and be shunted off to another home, to face yet another rejection, to have to worry so about who would love her, keep her, who would take care of her, on whom she could depend to never leave her, or, if she'd ever have her own home again. I would reach and touch her then, and she'd smile at me, but the smile was tremulous and she would quickly look away from me.

"Norma Jeane, my darling," I said to her. "This will not last much longer. I'll get home far more often than fighting soldiers do, so we'll be together a lot. And when I get home for good, we can start our family right away. Imagine, Norma Jeane, our own babies. Lots of them! I love you, Norma Jeane."

And her eyes would fill again, and she would turn and go back to packing up our life into corrugated cardboard cartons.

Finally, it was here. Norma Jeane was permitted to go down to the pier at San Pedro to see me off, which, if I'd been in the military, she'd never have been allowed to do. I felt proud because she was only one of three or four wives who'd come to see their men off. Maybe the other sailors' wives had said their good-byes at home, but for us, every second together mattered. It appeared to me that my Norma Jeane cared more than the other wives and it made our parting sweeter in a way, and therefore harder.

We stood on the dock at San Pedro. I held my dear, young wife to me and she sobbed softly against my shoulder for a few moments, and then I pushed her gently away and walked up the gangplank. It felt as if part of my body was cut from me and was being left there on the dock. I turned and looked back at her, my eyes filled with hot tears. She raised her hand. I could see the tears on her face. I never loved her more. I waved goodbye and walked into the ship. There were no hysterics.

We didn't realize then that I'd be gone for nearly a year, and that Norma Jeane, who always wanted to keep busy accomplishing something, would eventually become bored staying with my folks, and would soon desire to have a job.

Mom had been working at the defense job at Radio Plane and got Norma Jeane a job there also, a few months before I came home on leave. Mom worked in the company infirmary, and Norma Jeane first in the chute room on an assembly line. She became bored with that and so was moved to the dope room where they sprayed a liquid plastic, a stiffener (or dope) onto the cloth which was then made into the fuselage for the small target planes which flew by remote control and were used as targets for training aerial gunners as well as anti-aircraft units. It was started by Reginald Denny, the actor.

As I get older and look back over my life, I realize how everything in life, every happening is just one more link in life's long chain; that life is also like a jigsaw puzzle with all the pieces falling into place until finally, at the end, on the very last day of your very last breath, the puzzle is completed. When Mom got the job for Norma Jeane at Radio Plane, it was a precipitating event which put her into the exact spot where she'd be charmed away from the life we had together. The fates were set in motion and without my knowing it, I was fading to black, just like a scene in a movie. And there was nothing I could do about that.

Nothing at all.

CHAPTER 17

It was called the Liberty ship and it would make a long haul the first time out. The work was hard, but keeping busy kept me from feeling the pain of being without my Norma Jeane. We made for Townsville, Australia and then on to Milne Bay, New Guinea.

When we laid anchor there for nearly a month while awaiting orders, I had a lot of time to write to Norma Jeane, which I did, prolifically. And, after a wait of about three weeks, her letters came to me. I was so happy. There was a bundle of them, since she'd written to me every single day since I'd left.

They were sweet love letters. I'll never forget them. I'll never forget how they made me feel as I sat in what privacy I could find on a ship filled with men. Norma Jeane wrote of how she loved me, missed me, needed me. She told me how she missed meeting me on the corner after work, walking back to our apartment where we'd talk and laugh and discuss the day's happenings, how we'd greet Muggsie and play with her, play together. I'd hold the letters against me, pretending it was Norma Jeane. It was the only way I could touch her then, and it mattered to me out there. It mattered a lot.

And then, finally, my first leave. There she was, waiting for me at the Glendale Depot. We embraced and it was like an explosion. We crashed together. She was laughing, and then we were both crying. We galloped to my car and drove to the most luxurious motel lodge on Ventura Boulevard. I'll always remember the name--La Fonda. We had our meals sent in to our room, and we stayed there and hardly ever went out.

I'll never forget the black net nightgown Norma Jeane had bought just to please me. My God, she was spectacularly beautiful and sexy. She dazzled me. I loved her so and just don't have the words to express how my heart felt during that month. When we finally surfaced and went out to a restaurant one evening for dinner, we sat in the booth hugging each other, holding tight, making love as legally as we could in public.

In mid-hug that night I glanced over Norma Jeane's shoulder and saw an old girlfriend seated fairly near us. She was with her husband, a man I knew was a good deal older than she and they were in the middle of a terrible and loud fight. She struggled to smile at me. I knew she was embarrassed to be seen like that and I felt so sorry for her. She turned to her husband and in a sad voice we could all hear, said "Why can't you be sweet to me like Jim is to Norma Jeane?"

I knew this guy hadn't gone into the service yet, and so, my arms still around Norma Jeane, I smiled and said, looking straight at the girl, "If he had been gone a full year like I've been, he'd probably be a darn sight nicer to you than he is right now!" Norma Jeane put her hand to her mouth and giggled quietly. She knew the girl and that I'd dated her in highschool.

Finally, joking that we had to get out into the air and sunshine for at least a short time, we left the motor lodge and went horseback riding. Again! Norma Jeane wasn't scared, even though she remembered the incident when we went last time. This time, we rode out near the east end of the San Fernando Valley. The bridle trail crossed a stream and when Norma Jeane's old horse waded in, he put his head down, trying to drink and began to paw at the water. That's a surefire sign a horse wants to roll.

"Kick him, Norma Jeane!" I yelled. "Kick him in the side and get out of there. Make him go on!" But that old nag just lay down in about six inches of water.

Norma Jeane just casually stepped off him, as if she'd done it hundreds of times before and stood on the bank, her arms folded, waiting for him to get back up. Finally, the horse had had his nice roll in the water, and got back to his feet. I watched, laughing, as Norma Jeane sloshed back out into the water, climbed back on board and we rode off.

"Well," she said, looking over her shoulder at me, "at least I've got a cool horse!"

There was no TV in motor lodges back then, and so after we'd gotten reacquainted in the happiest of ways, we'd occasionally go out to see a movie. I recall so well one night when we were at Grauman's Chinese Theater and we were seated, kissing each other. A woman sitting behind us began to kick at the back of our seats.

Norma Jeane turned to look at her. "What's the matter with you?" she asked, and she was not especially polite, either.

The woman glared at her. "If you want to do that, why don't you go home?"

I saw Norma Jeane's eyes blaze in anger. "If I want to do this with my husband," she hissed at her, "then I will do it and furthermore, I will do it wherever I want to!"

With a great show, the woman got up and stalked out of the theater. Norma Jeane stayed angry for a long time that night. "Who does she think she is?" she kept saying. I laughed and hugged her more.

We would sometimes go to see friends during our month together, but Norma Jeane always preferred to be alone with me, and she still loved to park the car anyplace, any time to pitch woo, to neck, to make love. She never ever missed an opportunity, and created them where none existed. We simply could not get enough of each other, and it was like that for the entire month. I was a tired man during that time, exhausted, but a very happy man. I'll never forget that month with my Norma Jeane. I remember every single moment.

But, as leaves do, the time sped by and we were close to the end, close to the time I'd have to leave her again. Norma Jeane had begun to lose her zest. She'd phoned Radio Plane to tell them she was ill so she wouldn't have to lose any of her pay while I was home. She had earned the sick days. But she was getting tired. We'd been running around so much--

dancing at the Grove, trying every single bone rattling, dizzying ride at the Ocean Park amusement park in Santa Monica, taking long drives to places as far away as Death Valley, and again, horseback riding for long hours.

I realized how worn out my young wife was one late afternoon when we'd begun to horseback ride and it soon became dark. I turned back to Norma Jeane and said "Hey Darlin', it's getting dark. Turn your horse's headlights on." Her small tired voice came back to me. "Where are they?" she asked. "Right there, in front of your saddle," I laughed, but took her home. She was running out of steam.

The days narrowed down, and it was obvious to me that a kind of dread was engrossing Norma Jeane. She was becoming quiet, withdrawn--she would not talk or think about that dreaded day when I'd have to leave her again.

She was feeling fragile and very vulnerable as our time to part began to speed toward us. And suddenly, quite out of the blue, she decided to call her "father." Was it because I was leaving? Did I in some way represent the loving father she had always so dearly wanted? Whatever was in her mind, she'd decided that now was when she wanted to do it.

Norma Jeane and I had discussed her so called "illegitimacy" several times, although I'd always made it clear to her that the word was abhorrent to me--what baby, what child is illegitimate? None. Children are a gift, not an illegal issue, not to be branded for life because their parents did not marry.

However, I never had a sense that Norma Jeane was bitter about her situation. Without my knowing it, she'd apparently tracked down this man through people who had once worked with her mother at Consolidated Film Industries, where he and her mother had the affair which had resulted in Norma Jeane's birth. Did it bother or upset me that she'd done this detective work without telling me? No. It made me feel proud that this very young woman had the curiosity and brains and courage to try getting this information all on her own. Norma Jeane constantly surprised me. Finally she'd found her father and finally she found the missing piece of her life puzzle. His name was C. Stanley Gifford.

And so, finally, on that sad night, close to the time when I'd have to leave her again, with my mother sitting on the livingroom sofa and me standing next to her, Norma Jeane called Mr. Gifford, her father.

"This is Norma Jeane," we heard her say in a tiny, trembling voice. My heart ached so for her and I put my arm around her. "I'm Gladys' daughter," she said, and she sounded like a child, so guileless and scared.

No more than two seconds passed. Norma Jeane slumped and hung up the phone.

"Oh honey," she said, her eyes locked on mine, "He hung up on me," and she began to weep softly but that soon turned to wrenching, hollow sobs. I thought my heart would shatter to pieces for her. I led her back to the sofa and sat down next to her. Mom kissed her softly and quietly left the room.

"Sweetheart," I said to her as gently as I could. "Let's try to think of this man's point of view. You came at him completely out of the blue. Maybe we should have somehow given him a little advanced warning. You know, he disappeared from your mother's life and he's probably got another family now. You shocked him, honey. Maybe if some other time we give him a little warning, he'll act differently." I said these words to her as she sat, collapsed against me as gently as I could, and I know I didn't walk in his moccasins and that I should always try to put myself in the place of others but in my heart, I would have liked to kill the bastard at that moment for treating my dear wife so cruelly.

I was her husband, lover, and yes, her father figure. Yes, I know psychiatrists would have had a field-day with this situation, the Electra complex incarnate. But all of us marry for our own reasons, reasons hidden from our very souls sometimes, but that doesn't preclude the marriage being a good one. So what if I represented a father figure to Norma Jeane. So what? Ours was a strong marriage, based on trust and love and everything important. We loved one another dearly. If over the years, the pundits and arm-chair shrinks have deduced that Norma Jeane/Marilyn Monroe always sought out older men to fill the fatherless void in her life, again--so what? If people are happy and can make the ones they love happy in a sometimes very short life, then please, what's the big problem?

I read in Fred Lawrence Guiles's book "Norma Jeane," that years later Marilyn suddenly on impulse drove to her biological father's home with a friend. She'd discovered he owned a farm just outside of Hemet, a rural village near Palm Springs. Her friend asked her if she'd been in touch.

"Oh no," Marilyn was supposed to have said. "That's the whole point. I'm going to his farm to see him, to talk to him." So once again, Norma Jeane was planning on blind-siding this man, taking her alleged father by surprise, completely setting herself up. I wish I'd been there. I know I could have talked her into doing that in some other way--- some way that would maybe have been more successful.

But, apparently on the trip there, she had a change of heart stopped the car and decided to call him and not just arrive on his front doorstep.

Again from the Guiles book; "Hello," Marilyn said into the phone. "Is Mr. Gifford there?"

"Who's calling?" said a woman's stern voice.

"This is Marilyn. I'm his child...I mean, the little girl from years ago. Gladys Baker's daughter. He's sure to know who I am."

"I don't know who you are," the woman said, "but I'll tell him you're on the phone." There were minutes of silence. Finally, the woman came back on again.

"He doesn't want to see you," she said. "He suggests you see his lawyer in Los Angeles if you have some complaint. Do you have a pencil?"

"No," Marilyn said, her vice soft and low. "I don't have a pencil. Goodbye."

And I also wish I could have been there to hold her again, to ease the hurt. She must have felt murdered inside. God I wish I could have held her then.

But in some small way, maybe Marilyn got her revenge later on. As reported in the Guiles book, some ten years later when Marilyn was in the hospital for some routine surgery, she received an expensive silk embossed greeting card. It was signed "Best wishes for your early recovery. From the man you tried to see nearly ten years ago. God forgive me."

Apparently, Marilyn never answered the card, and one can only speculate her father's reason for sending it. Was he truly remorseful? Or was he thinking he might be able to cash in on what he hoped might be his very famous daughter's fortune? He'd have been very disappointed. Marilyn Monroe never kept any money she made, and she never made a great deal anyway. It was too little too late for C. Stanley Gifford. He had had his chance to save his little girl, to fill in that empty place in her life, and he rejected her. Thanks to him and other circumstances, Norma Jeane spent a lifetime being and fearing being rejected. These are the times I wonder about life after life, and if we do get to confront those who have damaged us. I wonder what Norma Jeane said to her father when they met in the afterlife. I wonder if she forgave him. My Norma Jeane had a tender, sweet heart and I suspect she forgave C. Stanley Griffith, although frankly in my opinion, he didn't deserve that sort of kindness from her.

After that night when Norma Jeane tried to call her father and he hung up on her, we became closer than ever. The days we could be together became fewer and fewer, and eventually, the terrible time came when we had to be parted again. It was such an awfully emotional time for her--for me too, but for her mostly. Such a sad, sad experience. Sad for me because it killed me to have to leave her, and sad for her because each time I left her, it was as if something terrible and hard just simply slammed into her, wrecking her, taking her down. Parting was not such sweet sorrow for us--it was devastating. Norma Jeane desperately needed something or someone to always be available, someone she could hold onto all the time. I remember whenever we were out together, even if we just went to a movie, she constantly had a tight grip on my arm or my hand--just as she had on our wedding day. She held on for dear life. And it was for her dear life that I let her.

The month was over. I left. Once again I was in the Far Pacific, and Norma Jeane went back to work at Radio Plane. She worked there so hard and with such dedication, they awarded her a big cloth "E" for excellence to hang on the wall. She was very proud of herself, and with good cause. That kind of thing was a very big deal for those dedicated workers.

It was very soon after Norma Jeane's starting work at Radio Plane that another piece of the jigsaw puzzle that was Norma Jeane's life clicked into place. A military photographer from Yank magazine, sent by actor Ronald Reagan, came through the plant on an assignment to take propaganda pictures of the girls at work there, "for the cause," he said. That photographer spied Norma Jeane, recognized immediately that she'd be a wonderful subject and he snapped the first historic photograph of her displaying some of her work at Radio Plane. That photographer could not possibly have known that that one small click of his camera was the beginning of Norma Jeane's new life, and the end of one I'd come to love. A simple click of a camera shutter and my life with Norma Jeane was in deadly jeopardy, on a slippery slope of such steepness, there would never be any way we could get back to the top. We tried, briefly, I struggled to do that more than Norma Jeane, but we could not recover from this. She in fact, didn't really want to. There was, as they say, suddenly stardust in her eyes and she became blind to the real world.

In an explosion, in rapid succession, Norma Jeane was being offered modeling jobs, many of them, and she grabbed at them. She kept working at Radio Plane, but all of her spare time was given over to the new pursuits of her life. It's been said that she had an affinity for the camera like no others had, or have, and all the photographers who worked with her knew that. Norma Jeane turned on to the camera lens, as if she'd been born to be in front of it. She'd light up as if someone, something, had thrown a switch inside of her. She'd glow. Much has been made of all this, but it is absolutely true. Even in the casual family snapshots taken of Norma Jeane, she reacts to the camera like no one else in the shot does, and no matter how many other people there are in the photograph with her, the eye just goes straight to her.

I'll never forget one home-coming. Norma Jeane showed up late--very late, driving my car--and telling me she was "so sorry, Jimmie, but I was on a modeling job and couldn't get away in time."

"Well, Darlin'," I said, "you're here. That's all that matters to me," and I pulled her into my arms. Norma Jeane kissed me, we embraced, but it had a vague, unexpected coolness to it--not very distinct, but it was there and I knew it and it pushed something sharp into my heart. I pulled back and looked into her eyes. But she just smiled and I told myself it was all my imagination—a reaction to the fatigue of my long trip. I told myself. I told myself.

This time, my leave was for only two weeks, which was just as well. I could have worked it to stay longer, but Norma Jeane was gone so much. She'd finally quit Radio Plane because her modeling jobs were coming so fast, both day and night, so we only had three of four evenings together during those two weeks. It was not enough, and I told her that, but all she would do is stare at me silently. There would be no budging her and I'd begun, finally, to reluctantly understand that.

I knew then as I know now that Norma Jeane never deceived me, just as I believe that she was always faithful to me. I know she'd been secretive at the first about the modeling jobs, but she had not lied to me about it. I mean, I hadn't asked about it because I didn't know about it, so she never actually lied about having this work to do—she just sort of didn't volunteer the information right away. Maybe she thought I'd "forbid" her or something, or that I'd take away this wonderful opportunity. And as I think back about it now, she wanted to keep this new thing secret for a while, like a wonderful new toy or possession. It was so new to her, a distant dream realized, that she couldn't talk about it. I think she was afraid if she told anyone, that big, beautiful, increasingly glittered bubble would, could, might burst on her and leave, the way so many of the beautiful, secure things in her life had been temporary and had disappeared.

No. In all the years she and I were so close, I know she never lied to me. Never. It just wasn't her thing. She hated to be lied to and admired honesty in people above nearly all else. For example, if Norma Jeane had been dating other men while I was away, she could never have kept it to herself--she would have felt compelled to tell me, at whatever cost.

And anyway, I'd have eventually seen a photograph of her on a particular modeling job taken during the time she'd been working. She was in so many magazines back then--on the covers, on the pages inside, in ads, not in ads, pushing makeup and shampoos, clothing, shoes, even cars and the parts thereof. It was just amazing to me. I'd always thought she was the most beautiful thing my Irish eyes had ever seen, but now, apparently, so did the world--or at least a small but rapidly growing part of it.

I never went on any modeling jobs (or "shoots") with her. I told myself it was none of my business, but as I think about it now, I really think that it would have made me feel uneasy--maybe jealous, seeing her pose and strut for a strange photographer, showing him her beauty, pushing her beautiful body at him, at the cameras. I also thought it might make her feel uncomfortable, having me there, it might cramp her style, keep her from being able to pose, to model as well as she could. And so I stayed away, my feelings jumbled and confused.

Norma Jeane began to have less and less time for me--and for Muggsie, too. He began to look ratty and unkempt. She never bathed him any more. I will always remember poor Muggsie lying on the porch all alone, staring up at us with sad eyes, knowing he was neglected, not loved any longer, not needed. Muggsie and I were beginning to have a lot of the same feelings.

And as for me, I know Norma Jeane was very aware that I was completely faithful to her while I was away. And it wasn't always easy. My memories of those times in foreign port are still strong; sex was for sale everywhere, and it wasn't always hidden. I remember seeing one of my buddies, sitting at a table, totally drunk while a girl unzipped his fly, and climbed on his lap, straddling him. The poor guy had a massive orgasm which nearly knocked him over backwards, his eyes rolling nearly up into his brain. I thought I'd choke to death laughing.

Things like that went on all the time, and they certainly had an effect on me, and on every man there. Every port offered every possible pleasure, but I didn't indulge myself. I couldn't. I'd never have been able to face Norma Jeane if I'd had sex with anther woman.

And then, after being in these wild ports, I'd come home and find myself no longer the center of her attention, of her world, as it had always been on my other leaves. Now when I'd come back, I'd get a distracted greeting from her (she was always late, if she bothered to show up at all) and I'd sit around being ignored and occasionally shoved into a tiny corner of her very busy day. I began to feel great resentment, greater sadness. It was all slipping away from me and all I could do was helplessly watch it happen.

CHAPTER 18

After our divorce, I married a good woman named Pat, and she presented me with the really best things in my life, the most important things--my three daughters. Nothing has ever given me so much joy. These children were--and remain--perfect. They have never stopped making me proud, giving me joy, and making me feel important and necessary. And loved.

At long last I had the family I'd yearned for. It was not with Norma Jeane, but she'd gone on to her other life and I to mine. We were both content with our lot in life.

Pat was extremely jealous of my former wife, and so it was for her I destroyed the love letters Norma Jeane had written to me. There were over 200 of them. I was tempted to keep them and of course, there was no way back then I could have known how incredibly valuable they'd be one day. Those letters and a few snapshots were all I had of my years with Norma Jeane, the only evidence and proof of her love for me, her strange, unpredictable moods, her dependency on me. But I knew how Pat would feel if she knew they were around and so I destroyed them. Pat would have thought I was clinging to the memory of my first marriage. Maybe she'd have been right.

Do I regret that I eventually destroyed all her letters? Of course. From a financial standpoint, it was a foolish mistake, but then, I don't know if I'd ever have been able to really sell them because I'd never have been able to forget how important they were to me when I was so far from my dear wife. But surely, they'd have given me a rather comfortable financial safety net, if I'd ever needed one. But as it was, I had to destroy them because another person was involved then, my second wife Pat, and it was important that I be sensitive to her feelings. But I do remember my joy in getting those letters, often bundled together, and I'd spread them out on my bunk by date and read her words to me and they gave me joy and warmth in my heart and I would think about how lucky I was to have this shimmering lady in my life. I remember how she'd write to me of her desperation, her loneliness, how she missed our being together, how she missed my touch, our sexual unions, how she was loving me loving her, our loving together, that she was being faithful.

I remember Norma Jeane's quoting a popular song to me in one of her letters;

I'll walk alone

 Because to tell you the truth, I'll be lonely.

I don't mind being lonely

When my heart tells me you are lonely too.*

My being away didn't deter her from buying me gifts, which she'd send to me, to wherever the mail caught up with us. One time I opened a package to find a handsome shaving kit which she had filled with Roi-Tan cigars. For someone so young, she was astonishingly thoughtful and sensitive. She enclosed a note with the cigars:

"Each time you smoke a cigar, darling, think it's a kiss from me. Ha ha!! Norma Jeane." She made me feel so loved. Until I got back home.

CHAPTER 19

Sometimes, I think, when we wonder why a person does something so different from the norm, so outré, it's good to try to put ourselves into their place, see the thing through their eyes. If we at least do this, or at least try to, we can perhaps gain some sort of understanding, some modicum of insight. And then sometimes, we can perhaps know why this person we may never have suspected of harboring such desires, does, in fact harbor them.

How seductive it must have been for this young, lonely child-woman, Norma Jeane Dougherty, to have suddenly been offered a glamorous, exciting new life as a model, an actress, to have enough money to never have to worry again. How bewitching to have these promises made to her. She would be taken to these glorious places, they told her, by the use of a simple, everyday device--the camera.

Yes, she was married to me, an older man, but still, she looked virginal, and very innocent. And looking that way has always been a turn-on to men. The glow that Norma Jeane possessed beamed from Marilyn Monroe, too, as a sort of translucence, like a window pane, frosted, with the light of a dawn shining through it. I know that sounds flowery, corny, but really, it's how she was. It's hard to explain. I've really never seen this --this sort of quintessence, on or in any other woman. Norma Jeane was lit as if by candles, within and without, and she had a stunning attraction to a camera lens. The combination was irresistible, irreplaceable, indescribable.

I don't think Norma Jeane was able to take a bad picture. She was completely free before that lens, open, sweet. Dressed or half dressed or undressed, Norma Jeane looked like an innocent, chaste young woman, utterly free of guile, with an overpowering need to be protected, another combination powerfully sexy and appealing to men.

The army photographer knew he'd found something special. Suddenly, Norma Jeane Dougherty was being told that she no longer had to be a simple little housewife working at a simple little job. Glittering things were being dangled in front of this young woman, things she only dreamed of when she was a girl. A woman sent her information about a modeling agency with a promise that she could simply not fail.

This woman's name was Emmeline Snively. She contacted Norma Jeane early in December of 1945, telling her the photographer André de Deines was looking for a female model to travel all the way up to Washington state with him for some western setting poses in the out of doors. We needed the money and coincidentally, the amount they were offering to pay was exactly the amount of money we needed to replace the motor of our 1935 Ford which had burned out.

"Do you want to go?" I asked her. She hesitated.

"No. Not really Jimmie, but I guess I should. We do need that money and I really should help out, to kind of contribute more to our lives. This guy is really a famous photographer Jimmie, and frankly it would be awfully good for my career."

Her "career" again. I was beginning to hate that word. But we were desperate, and so the week before Christmas, Norma Jeane went off with de Dienes. I met him and he seemed decent enough, a nice sort of guy. But he'd be traveling with my Norma Jeane, and I'd seen how men reacted to her, how they seemed to be unable to resist the temptation to touch her, be with her, to bask in that glow thing she had. And now my dear little wife was going off with this guy to make some money. I was extremely uneasy about all this, but decided to take the high road and to trust that everything would be fine. And so she left. Our parting wasn't exactly the passionate, tear-filled partings of before, when I had to leave for the Merchant Marine, but they were sad. For me sad, for her---well, let's just say that when the day came for her to go, she wasn't concentrating too hard on me.

She tried, truly she did, but her heart had begun to be elsewhere.

I was having dinner with Aunt Ana on Christmas day when the phone rang. It was my wife and my heart immediately ached when I heard her voice. She was crying.

"I want to come home, Jimmie," she sobbed.

"Well Darlin'," I said, "you just come on home. Come home now."

She was crying so hard it was very difficult to understand her, but eventually, I got the words.

"I can't, Jimmie. Most all of Andre's camera equipment was stolen and it was all my fault because I left his car unlocked. I'm responsible. And anyway, he hasn't paid me, probably because of this, and maybe he won't. I just don't know. Jimmie, I just can't come home until I have the money to fix the car. I can't come home but I want to. Oh, I want to Jimmie." It broke my heart to hear her sobs.

"Then what do you want to do, Norma Jeane?" I asked her. She didn't know.

Two days later, de Dienes dropped her off at Aunt Ana's. He did not walk her to the door the way a real gentleman would have. He just dumped her off.

When she came in, Norma Jeane would not speak of that time with de Dienes, but she did say she would never pose for him or be alone with him again. My imagination got the better of me when she said that, and I felt impotent, helpless. Enraged. But he had in fact paid her, so at least we got the money to get the car fixed.

CHAPTER 20

When she was Marilyn, Norma Jeane spoke of the times she'd spent at the movies as a kid, how she would go there when she was not welcome at whatever home she was living in at the moment. She spoke of how she'd stay in the movie house and see the same film again and again, and would be dazzled by the glamorous women movie stars on the screen--by their clothes, their make-up, their beauty. Did she want to be one of them? What little girl hasn't wanted that?

But was a hidden desire to be a model or eventually an actress smoldering deeply in her heart? A desire no one knew of? Her foster sister Bebe Goddard says that when they were together, they'd speak of such things, pretend and plan, scheme and dream, but again, what young girl didn't back then? Or even now?

I never knew it. No one in my family ever heard Norma Jeane say anything about these things.

So who knows? What I do know is that Norma Jeane was lonely for me while I was gone, and suddenly, this miraculous gift of promised glory and riches and the possible endless love of millions was offered her. Who could not be stirred and captivated by this? She was. Who could resist this? She was one who could not.

I won't speculate on what might have been. I wish I could have heard the first click of that first camera, the one that utterly changed my life forever, but I was thousands of miles away. And even had I been there, could I have stopped destiny?

CHAPTER 21

After that episode, life settled down to a routine for Norma Jeane while I was gone. She often wrote to tell me how much it meant to her to get my letters. It was forbidden that we tell our families where we were sailing, so Norma Jeane and I had worked out a code before I left.

One of the codes, for example, was this; if I began a letter with "Dearest," it would mean I was in New Guinea. We had dozens of codes, all meaning where I was writing from.

Norma Jeane and my mother went to work at Radio Plane every morning, and things were amicable between them. They'd make up their lunches together and would frequently shop together. And as long as our dog Muggsie slept on the back porch, my mother began to accept her, too.

My mother was awfully amused at Norma Jeane's naiveté and often told the story of driving by a bar after work, with a sign outside saying "Cocktails."

"Come on," Norma Jeane said to my mother one day as they passed the bar. "Let's go on in and get couple of cocks." My mother didn't laugh at her, and patiently explained that she didn't have it quite right and that she should really avoid using that term in the future.

CHAPTER 22

The end of us was nearing. I knew it. I wouldn't let myself think about it much, but when reality set in, I'd tell myself that it was happening. It was inevitable, and I could feel my heart slowly breaking. Norma Jeane was again being asked to go out on more and more modeling jobs. They were turning my young wife's head and I was powerless to stop the process. And, she was being told that she had a very good chance of becoming an actress. An actress! In the movies! She could be just like the magical, glamorous women she'd stared at up on the screen!

We had two wonderful war years together, but I had to keep leaving, and when I left, when they sent that photographer to Radio Plane and he saw her, he saw how young and beautiful she was, so sexy, innocent, vulnerable, -- in other words, when he saw all that had been mine, ours, when he looked through the lens and clicked the camera, Norma Jeane's journey began to begin. Ours began to end.

Norma Jeane used to take the old Ford I'd left behind and drive to Aunt Ana's house in West Los Angeles. The old woman was becoming more important in Norma Jeane's life, a trusted confidante. Quite soon, Norma Jeane would again move in with her, just as she had when the Goddards left for West Virginia, before she and I married each other.

Norma Jeane was seeing her mother more often, also, but their relationship was oddly strained, perhaps because Norma Jeane never really knew when her mother would "flip out" again, making her think that maybe one day she too, would be given to wild mood swings, unreasonable temper fits, deep sadnesses, thoughts of and plans for suicide, and crazy, aberrant behavior--which in fact is exactly what she did begin doing quite soon after she became

Marilyn Monroe.

But Aunt Ana knew that Norma Jeane was planning on a modeling career, perhaps a film career. She knew that Norma Jeane was beginning to wonder if marriage really was the thing for her. When I tried to speak with Aunt Ana about Norma Jeane's plans for her future, I never got too far. She acted in an awe-struck kind of way about it all, excited that Norma Jeane might become a movie star. I've always been very curious as to why Americans--well, perhaps it's people everywhere--get so air-headed on the issue of movie stardom. We treat movie actors as if they've got royal blood, as if they're right up there with world leaders, maybe even higher. Maybe divinely born. I think "stars" get more hoopla and adoration directed toward them than some world presidents do, than some of our greatest healers and scientists and religious leaders, and that's not good. Actors are just actors, entertainers. That's all. They are not gods, they have no more or less intelligence than anyone else.

But then, it's no wonder they begin to act as if they are divine beings, the way we worship them. My Norma Jeane began to get a taste of that as her career began to rocket forward.

As I was heading back to San Francisco and another shore leave, I received another letter from Norma Jeane, one of her very last to me. It was short, as short as a note one would write reminding a family member to pick up milk.

"Muggsie died," it said. "She wouldn't eat." I still think that dear dog died of a broken heart, from neglect. I know Norma Jeane loved Muggsie, but when I was around, that dog got groomed, bathed, fed and pampered constantly. Now, she was left alone all day while Mom was at work and while Norma Jeane was out on her modeling jobs. Dogs can do that--they can and do just fold up and die when they sense that they are no longer important, no longer loved. His beloved mistress Norma Jeane, just didn't want him any longer. I was beginning to understand exactly how that felt.

I wanted to be with my wife during that leave, doing what normal couples do when they've been separated for months.

But Norma Jeane was distant now--she'd actually moved to another level of her life. She'd begun divorce proceedings.

Norma Jeane used to tell my mother everything that was going on with her new modeling career, about Emmaline Snively's modeling school, about her dreams and plans to be famous. Things began to get tense at home because my mother knew these things, but she knew I didn't, and she felt as if she were betraying me by not telling me of Norma Jeane's plans. My wife once asked my mother what she thought I might think about her becoming a model.

"I don't think Jim would like it," Mom told her. It wasn't the answer Norma Jeane wanted to hear. Things were getting touchy at home because of Norma Jeane's new career plans, so soon after that, Norma Jeane loaded up my car with her things, and moved in with Aunt Ana in West Los Angeles.

But still, I was averaging a letter about every other day from Norma Jeane. When I think about those days I know now that somewhere in her mind she regarded my leaving her after Catalina as another rejection in her life. But it couldn't be helped. Intellectually, she knew that, but still, she was emotional and never rational about such things. We'd begun to build a life together and suddenly, it seemed to vanish. Yes, she was surrounded by my family who loved her and would take care of her in my absence, but still, I was gone, just as her mother kept on being gone in her life, like the father who'd never been around for her at all. Perhaps she never forgave me for that. But it didn't matter, because something else had slipped into her life and it was time for her to slip me out of it.

I want to make it clear that I never once heard Norma Jeane blame her mother for being mentally unbalanced and for having to give her up. And she didn't blame me for being in the service and having to ship out. But she was wondering why circumstances in her life were "doing" it again to her. After Catalina, after the packing up and her moving in with my family, even with all of that, she thought, in her heart that she was once again being abandoned.

Was she feeling those rejections when she enrolled at the Snively modeling school? Was that school another desperate attempt to find something permanent now that she thought I was out of her life? Even though she knew I wasn't? I think so. It's very complicated. The military photographer at Radio Plane had been responsible for showing her that she had something to share with the world, something which would make so many people love her that if a few didn't it would not matter--there would be many, many more who would.

At first she did not even tell my parents she'd enrolled in the modeling school. She just told them that she would be busy for a number of evenings. But Norma Jeane must have known that being secretive with my family was an awful way to be, considering that they'd accepted and loved her from the start, and took her gladly into their home for the duration of the war, or until I got back home. They even took Muggsie as part of the deal.

Having secrets was not part of Norma Jeane's make-up. It was unnatural to her, and she was never easy about keeping secrets or lying, and so she did not. She and I had no secrets from each other--at least while we were together in the beginning. I remember that before we got married, Grace had advised her to tell me that she was illegitimate and had taken the name "Mortensen" because it was the one her mother had put on the birth certificate.

And so she did. Norma Jeane told me and also told me before our wedding that I could back out of the marriage if I wanted to. I'll never forget her face while she told me that. She was scared, but brave really. Her eyes were round and unblinking when she spoke. It made me feel sad, and very tender toward her. I knew it wasn't an easy thing for Norma Jeane to say. After all, "illegitimacy" was a very bad thing back then, something to be ashamed of, to keep hidden if possible. But she was too honest for that. She had to tell me.

"Norma Jeane," I said, and I was so emotional I had a hard time speaking. "How could that ever make any difference to me? I wouldn't back out of a marriage with you because of something like that. Always remember honey--you were a love child and babies don't have choices in these things-- they're just babies after all, things to love."

"But Jimmie," she said, "what about when we have kids of our own? What will we tell them?" She looked so distressed, so scared.

"Norma Jeane, if it ever comes up and it very well might, we'll just tell them to not worry about it, to not even think about it. And you know another thing? I think it just makes you that much more beautiful." Her eyes filled and she put her arms around me.

But in spite of her strong need for honesty, secrets were obviously starting between us, while I was away on ship- board. Norma Jeane was beginning her new life. If I'd been home or even if I'd been on a leave, we could have talked it all out, but I was not there and she couldn't tell my folks at first either. I'm not suggesting at all that she'd have aban- doned her dream or her new career, because Norma Jeane Dougherty always completed what she started, always went in to a new project with the idea of seeing it through com- pletely. But at least, had I known, we could have made some sort of plan about it. Together.

I know the modeling career was hard work for her. She was still working at Radio Plane, after all, and taking mod- eling classes at night, but it was a challenge and she had the courage to meet and conquer it. Norma Jeane was a deter- mined woman, strong minded and this life-choice was her own idea.

And even though later on, after she'd left me, the chal- lenges grew bigger and more impossible when she took her new name and threw herself into her new life. But still, she went for them with complete determination, and was al- ways grew more and more successful. And more and more alone.

I always wondered if Norma Jeane sometimes wished she could go back to being Mrs. Dougherty instead of being The Great MM; if she could go back to a place where no one wanted anything from her other than her friendship and love; if she could go back with a family who would be there for her always, where a problem could be solved by talking it over with family members, and that their advice would be sincere and without any hidden agenda. Where she'd be safe.

And so, I had to go back to sea and I knew this time, no one would weep for me. I'd signed the papers when I'd arrived home and eventually the papers were filed. I eventually received them in Manila. The 13th of September was the date of my final divorce papers and my discharge from the service.

The irony of the situation is that when the sailor who was giving out the mail handed me the letter, he saw the return address from a Las Vegas attorney, laughed and said, "Hey! Your old lady's divorcing you."

She definitely was. I thought about jumping over the side of the boat. I instantly thought about any way possible to kill myself.

But then, it was gone. All of it. The feelings flashed away from me just as quickly as they had started, like the waves of ocean water separating and splashing away from the bow of the boat as it sliced through the azure water. Long training, early years of introspection, long habits of dis-allowing feelings of self-pity steadied me immediately and I was again centered, focused. This would not kill me. I would not allow it to. I pulled in a huge breath, and I became calmed.

"Well," I thought. "This is baloney. There's no way I can get to her, talk to her. But there is one sure way I can let her know immediately that this letter has arrived."

I nearly ran to the captain.

"Sir," I said, "I want my wife's allotment cut off as of this second." He had a wireless sent from our radio right there in China, and presto! the allotment money was ended. Norma Jeane would not get a single penny more. It was a small victory and maybe vindictive. Some night say childish. Who cares what some might say? I didn't see much sense in spending my very hard-earned money on a wife who was not a wife any longer.

I'll never forget what she told me when I got back home. With her lower lip stuck out like a sulking child, she told me how she'd been living in a boarding house in Las Vegas and was in the hospital being treated for a terrible case of trenchmouth when she got the news. She told me how low she'd felt when she got that news, as sick as she was.

"Well gee, Norma Jeane," I said and I deliberately laughed at her as sarcastically as I could. "I'm so sorry I had that money cut off when you were sick. How thoughtless of me! Golly, I should have been more sensitive. Now, let's see here. Umm-- I wonder, Norma Jeane, since we happen to be on the subject of surprise letters, if you maybe gave any thought to my feelings when you had that letter sent to me on board ship."

She stared at me for a moment and then just looked away from me. She didn't answer. Of course, she couldn't. But, Norma Jeane had broken the rule about keeping her residence in Las Vegas for six weeks after she had the letter sent to me about the divorce. She was frequently going to Los Angeles on modeling jobs, and of course I could have proved this if I'd had the desire to contest the divorce. The pictures would have proved her residency rule beyond doubt.

But what was the point? Why contest a divorce with a partner who doesn't want to be married to you? Would contesting it have made her want to stay with me? No. Would it have made her love me enough to give up her dreams of fame and money and possible world-wide adulation? Hardly. I was then and am today a realist. I face facts when they are facing me. When she had the lawyer send me the divorce notice, I was quickly wounded but then I just as quickly began to heal. But I will admit that sometimes--- sometimes, the pain would flood back over me. But only sometimes. And even today it does, if I let it. Norma Jeane really did hurt me. There it is. I've said it. It is true and I won't say it again.

But eventually I did refuse to sign the divorce papers until she'd consented to have a long talk with me. I had to hear it directly from her own mouth. She had to convince me that it truly was over. I was unable to really believe it in spite of all that had happened. And so, until I heard her words, heard her say the words I was so afraid to hear, I would not be able to completely accept this. And yes, in the very smallest part of my heart, I prayed, I believed that when we were together again, I'd hold her to me, keep my arms around her and she'd realize that I was her protector, her mainstay, that she depended on me and always could--and eventually we'd get into bed together and everything would be wonderful again. Norma Jeane would be back with me, I would be back with her and our life together would continue and go on forever.

But no. It was not to be and I knew it. I did. And in fact as I look back--and what else have I but to look back--if in fact we'd stayed married and raised a family together, I know I'd look over at her from time to time and I'd see a longing in her face, a yearning in her beautiful blue eyes and I'd realize that she'd be thinking about her old dreams, wondering if she'd followed them if she'd have made it, if she'd have become a famous actress. And my heart would break for her and I'd wonder if I'd forced her away from the possibility of her being able to swing from a star and carry moonbeams home in a jar.

I stayed with my family during that next leave, and had to actually go to Ana's to "call" on my wife. I won't soon forget how I felt standing outside that house early that morning, waiting for Norma Jeane to answer the doorbell.

I'd driven up in a taxi to the Nebraska Avenue house where my wife was living. I saw my old 1935 Ford coupe parked in her driveway. It was early in the morning. I planned it that way so I'd be sure to find her home.

I'd been anxious to get out of my sailor uniform and had bought a suit the night before in Long Beach, right after we'd landed. They didn't have my size and the suit was too big, but I bought it anyway, knowing I really could have looked a lot better for the "reunion" between Norma Jeane and me. But I just didn't want to be wearing my uniform. I hoped for the best.

The door opened. Norma Jeane stood there gazing up at me, pulling a thin wrap around her. My heart began to feel squeezed. God she was so pretty even though she looked as if she had not slept very well at all. I looked into the room and saw her mother Gladys lying in the bed, our bed, in my place in the bed, looking anxious, as if afraid I'd make a huge scene because of the coming divorce, because her daughter was leaving me. I would not have. I was beyond scenes. I was trying to get beyond hurt.

"I think my mother's sort of upset," said Norma Jeane in a half whisper, nodding her head in her mother's direction just in case I hadn't noticed where she was sleeping. And then she looked me over carefully. A bit of the old twinkle I loved came to Norma Jeane's eyes.

"Your suit doesn't fit," she giggled.

"I know. But I wanted out of that sailor suit."

"Let's talk tomorrow," she said softly. "Maybe even a little later on today, Okay? Can we do it then Jimmie? Please?"

"Okay," I said. "Okay." I looked around the room, saw the car keys on a small table, walked over and put them into my pocket. Gladys stared at me, looking afraid. She knew I used to box in the service, that I used to kill animals for food when I was a kid and in her floating in-and-out nutsiness, I suspect she thought I was a serious threat to her and to Norma Jeane. I smiled at her and looked at Norma Jeane.

"I'll take the car," I said. "I'm gonna need it to get around during my leave." I confess to feeling a small but delightful sense of vengefulness in taking those keys, because I knew her not having the car would inconvenience her. I know it was childish, but causing her some discomfort made me feel good just about then. She'd dumped me. This woman I'd have taken a bullet for, would have died for, this woman I wanted to spend my life with, to mother my children couldn't even have the decency to let me know in her own words that she was going to leave me. She had dumped me with the words on a piece of paper from some lawyer. She couldn't even tell me herself. She didn't think enough of our time together to tell me herself.

But Norma Jeane had been a terrible driver anyway and so I sort of felt I was rescuing my old car from her. When I turned and looked at it parked in the street however, I was somewhat surprised to see that it was still in good shape, considering her terrible driving record.

Norma Jeane looked very surprised, but she didn't protest. After all, it was my car and she'd just simply taken it for her own use while I was overseas.

"Well," she said slowly, "I really do have to have--- umm — well, all right, Jimmie."

I stood looking down at her and again remembered what a terrible driver Norma Jeane had been. I'd tried hard to teach her, but she never seemed to get it that she really should look straight ahead when she was driving, and not out the side windows. That she'd have to forgo her natural curiosity about what was going on around her while she was driving. She'd forget that she had hold of the steering wheel. She'd wave her hands around, and talk or daydream or sing along with the radio as she drove and would get so involved she would forget to pay attention to what was in front of her. She was truly dangerous behind the wheel. Once she ran into a streetcar at a wide-open intersection with absolutely nothing around to keep her from seeing it coming. It's funny to speak of it now--but it could have hurt or killed her when she did that, and if I'd lost her like that my life would have also ended.

Norma Jeane had taken my car with her when she moved to Aunt Ana's, which of course made sense. I was thousands of miles away, and obviously had no use for it. But I was home now, and I was definitely going to take it back. I needed it too, after all.

I was also more than a little "honked" at Norma Jeane when I heard she'd quit Radio Plane, and without a reliable income, was using my allotment check to keep her in the clothes and make-up she had to have for her modeling work. To this day I don't understand why these agencies didn't buy the clothes and make-up for her. But they didn't. I did.

I walked away from her with the car keys in my hand.

"I think that soon I'll be making lots more money, Jimmie," she called after me. "I'll be getting much better fees."

I turned and tried to smile at her, but it wasn't a real smile, a healthy smile. I guess it probably looked more like a sneer.

"That's nice, Norma Jeane," I said. "I'm very glad for you." Norma Jeane looked at me. I could see that she was hurt by my coldness, but I really didn't care much. She didn't know the meaning of hurt, the way I did. The car was still in my name, after all. It was mine, not hers, and I was determined to not support her for one more instant. If she was not going to be my wife any longer, I was not going to be her meal ticket. She could do nothing about that. She sighed.

"Bye, Jimmie," she said, her voice small. "Sorry about this morning."

As I drove away, I thought "she's sorry about this morning? This morning? What about our whole life? What about the divorce? She's not sorry about the divorce?"

Even though I was good at putting pain out of my life, as time passed, it would come back in sometimes, when I didn't expect it, when I heard a song or saw a flower or looked outside and saw a beautiful day. At first, the pain of Norma Jeane's leaving me was a hard pain, hard like a chunk of split granite, hard like a knife. And that's how it felt for a moment as I drove away from her that morning. I began to think about not signing the divorce papers. Why? I didn't know then. Revenge? Obstinacy? Who knows. Probably. My mind was in a state of pained confusion.

Norma Jeane and I spent the next day together, doing a lot of talking, and it was then I was to discover to my utter amazement that she wanted to continue on with our way of life, to act as man and wife, live together, have sex, share a home, but, to be divorced. She wanted to live like a married couple, without being one.

The studios were romancing her, they were after her now, and one of the big ones told her that they would never take on a starlet for the intensive grooming and training programs that would, with hopes, lead her to stardom, if she were married. The studios invested a great deal of money making a young girl into a big star, and hopefully a "sex goddess" and couldn't take the chance that she'd get pregnant. Back then, don't forget, women usually got pregnant with a husband. (If they got pregnant with a man they were not married to and the public found out, the scandal would have ruined her. Her career would have been over. His? No. Of course not.) And don't forget--back then no woman could really be sexy if she were married. Found in the Gospel according to Hollywood, the minute a woman married, her sexuality drained from her like water from a leaky bucket.

Therefore, married starlets were verboten. And not only did marriage take away a young woman's sexiness, according to the great minds that ran the studios, if they got pregnant, even if they were married, they would no longer be seen as being sexy. Giving birth also robbed a woman of her sex appeal. They became instant "spoiled goods." Therefore, the huge investment the studio made in these young and hopeful girls was lost forever. What a crock. Some of the sexiest women alive are mothers and even grandmothers. But then, that's how I think. Back then people were perhaps a bit narrower of vision. Too bad.

Naturally I was upset about all this, but still found myself hoping we could work it out and remain married. I saw a faint ray of hope for us in her proposal. Weak, very faint, but that old cliché about "where there's life there's hope" and "hope springs eternal" buzzed around in my mind. I was hurting more than I could admit to myself and while I knew I'd survive this pain and be able to move on, I was hoping in the deepest part of my heart that Norma Jeane would reconsider.

And I hasten to add that I wasn't a prude then and I'm sure not now, but I have a certain credo, certain strong beliefs and one of them, as old fashioned as it seems today, was that a man and woman should be married to one another, especially when there are children involved. I wanted children. Norma Jeane said she did. I would not subject them to what I perceived as a weird situation where their parents were not married. I know it's done today and I don't much think about that or even care what people do. I have to live with myself and play by my own rules where this matter is concerned, and I simply could not be "with" Norma Jeane and not married to her.

And yes, perhaps you're thinking that I had some problem with perhaps being called Mr. Monroe. My ego isn't so fragile that I couldn't have withstood that, but who wants to lose one's identity that way? I know there are women who think their IDs are perhaps lost because they take their husband's family name and actually I agree with that. No one should have to give up who they are and get lost in another person unless it is his or her choice. But I'll tell you this---in my opinions, it sure makes life a whole lot less complicated if everyone could agree on one last name no matter whose it is, especially where children are concerned. To say nothing of names on mailboxes and in phone books! I guess it's all about choices though and all people should have the right to make whatever choices they see fit to make as long as no one gets damaged along the way. At least that's how I feel.

CHAPTER 23

My leave was up. I found out I had been assigned to a freighter slated to go to the China Sea.

Work on a freighter can be endless, backbreaking and always hard, but there are long periods of boredom, too. So I'd take that time, "down time" as they say today, my arms propped on the railing, and I'd stare out at the beautiful Pacific Ocean, thinking about Norma Jeane and how hard it was becoming for me to keep her, to hold her to me. Harder and harder each day for me to keep my endurance. It could almost be compared to holding back a beautiful animal who'd just discovered that it was a wild animal and it had begun to strain hard against its boundaries, or fences. I began, finally, to understand that it was just becoming impossible to try to hold her to me. I had to face the fact that she just didn't want to be held. She could no longer be restrained. What were once for her the joys of wifedom, homemaking, and possible parenthood were no longer joyous. Those "stations" of her life were now her obstacles and she had to be rid of them. I was losing my Norma Jeane and there was really nothing to be done about. Fame, the adorations of countless masses of people and the promises of big money were winning. Does it always?

Looking out over that huge ocean, I'd think about how different Norma Jeane had become, about the changes that had happened to her so swiftly. When we were married, she was so anxious to please me--as I was to please her. But that was all gone now. Well, at least gone from her. I'd have done anything to please her, especially if it would have meant keeping her. I'd have loved her and even worshipped her until the end of time. She would have been my primary focus. In fact I would have lived just for her. I know that sounds hopelessly romantic and not at all realistic, and I know I would have always lived a life I loved for myself too, but Norma Jeane Baker Dougherty would have been my sun, my moon and my stars and I would have devoted my life to her---just as I thought she would to me. Obviously I misgauged that one!

Norma Jeane had become calculating. She'd never been like that before. Never, and this "new wrinkle" amazed and angered me. It was so new in her, so odd, so totally out of character. And so confusing to me. I couldn't understand this trait in Norma Jeane, but I surely could see it now. Where had she hidden all this stuff when we were together?

When I got back home again, Norma Jeane told me her mother was being released from an institution up north. She wanted me to meet the bus when her mother arrived, and take her to stay with the Goddards who had returned to California from West Virginia. She'd stay there until I'd go back to sea and then she'd move in with Norma Jeane.

I agreed and remember being more than a little shocked at seeing Gladys again. She was vague, sort of polite, but just not connected at all. In that past, when she was having a good spell, she was in pretty good control of things. But not this time. Her mind was off in space somewhere and she just seemed to be floating, not focusing at all when she talked. She was all in white, the way Norma Jeane used to dress when our marriage was strong. (She stopped wearing white so much after her modeling days began because they told her it didn't photograph too well. But it seemed she picked the trend up again as the years went by--witness the famous scene of her standing over the subway grate in The Seven Year Itch. That dress, I read, gets sold and resold over the years, as does the famous "Happy Birthday Mr. President" dress.)

But that day, Gladys was wearing a completely plain white dress, nylon I think, and white shoes and stockings. She looked exactly like a nurse in uniform. I wondered if Gladys was trying to actually look like a nurse which I thought was pretty weird because she was a devoted Christian Scientist, very pious, and of course, they don't believe in or partake in any of the intelligence and healing abilities of the medical profession. It was so odd and gave me a creepy feeling, seeing Gladys like that, so white, so distracted, so not there. I worried for Norma Jeane. Would my darling be safe with this ghostly, strange woman who was her mother? I didn't know and I was very uneasy. Gladys always seemed to be trying to grasp at things that were never there. Ever. She never got angry. She never got happy. I do not ever recall seeing Gladys even laugh. Gladys stayed in this sort of misty limbo, unable or unwanting to cope. I guess she felt safe there.

But ah, she was a beautiful woman. She never did anything to her face to enhance that beauty, she never dressed beautifully. I would sometimes peer at her and think one day my Norma Jeane would look like that when she got to be that age, although I knew Norma Jeane would always do everything to enhance her beautiful God-given qualities. But then, my Norma Jeane never got to grow old, never got to become even middle-aged so I never knew if she would have become her mother.

Grace Goddard had gone with us that day to pick up Gladys, and when Gladys stepped down off the bus, the two women embraced passionately, extraordinarily happy to see one another. (An odd and instantly disappearing emotion for Gladys.) But when Norma Jeane greeted her mother, it was as if she were greeting a sort of friend--an oddball friend. She was careful, not letting herself get too close. This did not surprise me. After all, Norma Jeane never once visited her mother in the state hospital, at least not when we were married. And it's not that I blame her for that. I mean after all, Norma Jeane was always in a world of hurt where her mother was concerned so there was a danger in going to see her under any circumstances – and the danger was that her mother would reject her again, either by being off in lala land again or saying something to her daughter which would hurt her. Again. My darling, my tender Norma Jeane was hurt so much. I used to wonder if her poor heart was criss-crossed with scars from those hurts. I think it was.

I know other kids had it worse. I know other youngsters

have suffered horribly in life, but you know, there's no accounting for how individuals react to what life hands them. Some kids grow up in indescribable situations, so horrifying they cannot even be adequately described. And they become fine, upstanding, normal and strong adults, not even showing the scars of their childhoods. Other people can't do that. I guess it all has to do with the tenderness and fragility of each individual's inner-ness. Norma Jeane's reactions to her upbringing were all her own and she reacted by withdrawing, but holding people "hostage" by being everlastingly late to everything, by her uncontrollable mood swings, by her terror of becoming crazy like her mother, and always being chased by her demons and terrifying lonelinesses. My poor sweet beloved Norma Jeane.

I stared at the mother and daughter that day and thought how alike they looked. The bones in their faces were similar. Both women were so pretty, but as I said, poor Gladys never attempted to enhance her natural beauty. She kept herself as plain as she could, never bothering with make-up or having her hair done. I didn't know that day at the bus stop if Norma Jeane had as yet told her mother about our pending divorce.

I recall after I'd entered the service, Norma Jeane told me that she and Gladys had gotten close for a short while. Norma Jeane was always willing to give anyone the benefit of the doubt, and way down into her heart she truly wanted to forgive her mother and become a close, dear and good friend. But it wasn't easy, her mother being so "out there" and all, but, my sweet Norma Jeane was ever hopeful and ever willing to try to make it all come out right.

"After all, Jimmie," she'd say to me, "she's kind of like someone I really don't know because I was only a very little girl when she left me. I honestly can't ever remember thinking `this is my mother,' or anything like that, but I do try to remember the happy times. We'd go to the beach or we'd just visit with each other. I remember those times, Jimmie. They were so wonderful," and she'd look away, and I would know that those times could probably be counted on one hand, and yet my beloved wife clung hard to those wispy memories.

Grace Goddard and Gladys spent the day together that day after we picked Gladys up, kindly giving the time to Norma Jeane and me so we could talk, to try to get things worked out. The two women thought it could all get straightened out. My heart was already telling me it was hopeless, but I had to keep trying. I remember that day we spoke of so many things, but also, we talked a lot about money.

"I'll eventually be making a lot more money, getting more jobs and much higher fees," Norma Jeane would always say. And I'd have the unpleasant task of bursting her balloon by reminding her that all the money right then she was making was going on her back. Or on her face. No one was paying for (or even offering to pay for) all the clothing and makeup she had to have in order to pursue this new big career thing. God forbid she should wear something a little less expensive, or even something over again! Nothing but the finest for Norma Jeane, and "the finest," as everyone else seemed to understand, except her, costs.

If we were to stay married, I knew I'd have to make a lot more money now that those dollar signs were in my wife's beautiful eyeballs, and one way for me to do that was to go back to sea earlier than I'd planned. I'd seen that Norma Jeane had drawn all the money we had together out of our account and she was managing to spend my entire $170. a month allotment. I know that's a pittance by today's standards, but it stretched a lot longer back then. Still, she managed to spend every dime of it with absolutely no care about its belonging to both of us. But at least we did not have any car payments to make because I'd paid cash for that.

As we spoke that day, I remember being finally forced to realize that Norma Jeane was really not speaking about our financial future together as a couple, or our future together on any level. She was speaking only of her future in show business, in the modeling business. She seemed completely unconcerned about any dreams or plans of mine. She never asked me about any of that and it saddened me to recall how she and I had always talked at great length about both of our dreams and hopes. It was always "us" and "our." Now it was I, Me, Myself, My and Mine. The five "I Diseases." My beloved Norma Jeane was greatly changed now, concerned only with her wonderful new career and life and her new, beautiful clothes and the jobs she'd wear them to. And of course, those great big pie in the sky dreams of her becoming a world famous actress, beloved of millions, remembered and adored forever really overwhelmed her and kept her from thinking about anything much else---especially us. Well Norma Jeane my darling, I guess it wasn't so much pie in the sky because that's exactly what happened. Congratulations! You did it, Honey. But oh, the cost.

There were stacks of magazines in the house now, all with her picture on the covers or inside on the pages. She was so proud and was confused when I did not react as she wanted me to or thought I should---that I did not share the pride in her success, that it all sort of embarrassed me. And in all honesty, I was scared. Really frightened. I could see this new life was quickly pulling her away from me, farther and farther, faster and faster, and there was nothing I could do but just helplessly watch it happen. It was like watching a wave crashing to the shore that had engulfed me so lovingly and passionately for years, then quickly sliding away forever. It was the most helpless feeling for me--and feeling helpless was an emotion I was unused to. I was only 25, but Norma Jeane was only 20, and already a sort of celebrity. To say the least, I felt very, very threatened. And the sadness in my heart was like a large ball of hot lead. I am sorry to sound so melodramatic, but that's how it felt, and it hurt and it burned and it was eating me alive.

But, as I've said before, I was given a good sense of humor and perspective. These things were born in me, and have gotten me through some rough times in my life. I could always rely on them. I have always been able to recover—to pick myself up and dust myself off and start all over again, as the song says so well.

And yet, this was a period in my life when I lived on and for memories. Norma Jeane was distancing herself from me more and more as her fame grew and her modeling jobs increased. Sometimes I'd think there was hope for us because of things that happened, little situations or happenings which would cause me to grasp at those "hope straws." But those times were becoming just memories and they were disappearing fast the way smoke does in the wind.

I would remember sometimes, as all this was happening, about the time she told me when she was out on a modeling job, posing at an old turkey farm. After the posing was finished and the pictures all taken, she discovered she'd lost her engagement ring and wedding band. She told me how she'd gotten down on her hands and knees and had crawled about for a couple of hours, the photographer too, until they were finally found. This story gave me great hope that she still loved me, still wanted the marriage, but alas, no. It was another of those "smoke" things, another "hope straw." It didn't change her at all.

And so it all just wasn't working so well for us any more. I was on a slippery slope and the harder I struggled, the more I slipped down and down. I was losing my wife and the life I'd known and loved with her. I'd always enjoyed change--welcomed it in most ways. I considered myself a progressive young man--but there were things in my life I wanted to remain stable, and one was my marriage to this young, beautiful woman I loved beyond description. But it wasn't happening any longer and as I watched my marriage to Norma Jeane slip slowly away from me, I remember finally thinking, "Oh hell! This is no way to live."

And so, I had to go back to sea and I knew this time, no one would weep for me. I'd signed the papers when I'd arrived home and eventually the papers were filed. I eventually received them in Manila. The 13th of September was the date of my final divorce papers and my discharge from the service.

I was making my last trip overseas. The last trip. the last

of my marriage. It was the end of the beginning. I remember staring at a sunset one night from the railing of my ship, and finally, as it got darker, I felt myself sigh deeply and I pushed myself away from the railing. That tiny gesture was an oddly freeing movement for me. I remember it so clearly. I suddenly understood, no, I finally accepted that I was part of Norma Jeane's past now and there was no place for me in her future. None in the least. I understood also that she was perhaps willing to occasionally toss me some crumbs of affection, but I finally completely understood that I was not at all willing to settle for that. It was over. No more crumbs. No more straws. No more smoke. I went below.

CHAPTER 24

It was to be the longest week of my life, that leave in 1946. Norma Jeane was definitely going to leave me. I knew it totally now and was at some peace with it. But after all, I'm human and even though I had finally come to terms with it and accepted the inevitable, there was still once in a very great while, a tiny part of me hoping it would all get better, hoping our life together would just miraculously go back to the way it was. I knew it would not and those feelings only bubbled up occasionally. I was facing it.

I admit though that I thought a lot about Norma Jeane's proposal, living together without marriage. But eventually, as I knew it would from the start, I had to admit to myself that I just could not do it. I was very conventional back then (still am), not altogether rigid, but I had certain moral values and credos which I followed, and one of them was that I wanted to be married, to have children in the conventional way--marriage license, mom, dad, children, in that order. Oh well, I've already talked about that. Nothing's changed. I'm still a conservative traditionalist and I still believe in one name being on the mailbox.

And so I of course told her no. I had to tell Norma Jeane that I couldn't "live in sin," that we had to be married or not together at all. Honestly, I have never in the least bothered or concerned with people whose lifestyle differed from my own. It was only that I had certain perhaps old fashioned, ideas on how things should be--at least for me, and having a home and with a mother, father and kids around was one of my own personal "should be's." There I go again, repeating myself. I must be getting old!

But, all of that was fifty years ago and I've softened over the years. I think if all of this had happened to me now, I'd maybe have been able to roll with it. I'd have understood that I'd have had a frequently absent wife and I'd have gotten myself involved in many activities, charities, a business —volunteer work. She could go off, do her thing, I'd do mine, and we'd be together when we could. And who knows? It might have worked out. It sometimes does. Many of today's marriages work perfectly well in set-ups like this.

But back then, no. I wanted marriage in the old fashioned way. Her--home in the kitchen with our children. Me--out making a lot of money to bring home to the family I loved. Alas, it was not to be.

Norma Jeane and I spent all that next afternoon talking and talking. I was scared, apprehensive--really more about her than about me. I'd seen her through so much, knew her so well. I'd helped her through countless wild mood swings and strained circumstances. I'd seen her through her strange weirdnesses, her angers, terrors, dreads and unreasoning and unreasonable frights. I worried that she'd never be able to handle this big career thing on her own. I worried that strangers would take advantage of her sweetness and innocence. I worried. I was right to. From all I've read, Norma Jeane never really "toughened" to the world, and believed things about human beings in the most naïve way. I think she was probably taken advantage of right to the end. I think Norma Jeane was just too trusting. I think it helped to boggle her mind and to eventually contribute to her far too early death.

I began to ask her, that long afternoon, and all during the rest of that week, if she'd really carefully considered the step she was taking. Had she looked at all the angles? Was she absolutely sure?

Norma Jeane told me she'd been happy enough as my wife. My heart leapt in joy. Perhaps she was reconsidering! But no. My balloon burst when she followed that statement with "But please, Jimmie, sign the papers."

And so finally, Norma Jeane completely stopped speaking about our future together. All she could speak of was her career. I marveled over the fact that in the year and a half I'd spent at sea, she'd metamorphosed into this completely different woman--this other being. I remember how I'd stare at her, searching that glorious face for the soul and heart of the sweet young girl I'd left behind me, the girl who adored me, whom I adored--but she was gone. She still was called Norma Jeane Dougherty, but Norma Jeane Dougherty had vanished.

The next day we drove around everywhere together through the valley, and I can remember the pain in my heart as we revisited all the places we'd known as lovers. Between that-- and seeing how she'd made sure I'd see her mother Gladys sleeping on my side of our bed -- and hearing her words, well, it was not my finest hour. Her mind was set firmly. Norma Jeane Dougherty was going to be an actress.

"I always thought I was the family ham," I told her. "So how come you want to perform all of a sudden?"

"It's not all of a sudden, Jimmie," she said, her voice now cool, now very different. "I know it's hard for you to understand because I never talked about it with you, and I kept it -- well, kinda hidden. I don't know--maybe it all began when I spent all those hours at the movies. Seeing those ladies up there--so beautiful, glamorous--everyone loving them---"

And then, finally, she just stopped listening to me. Except to say to me, "I can't let this chance go down the drain, Jimmie. I've worked too hard." Norma Jeane had gotten some sort of "fever," given to her by that modeling agency that was after her, and by its owner, Emmeline Snively. That woman and her agency put those thoughts into the heads of their models.

And I'm quite certain that it was Ms. Snively and others in the modeling and movie business who urged Norma Jeane to divorce me, who convinced her that I, as a husband, was expendable, and would only hold her back.

Truly I blame no one, however. I mean, no one put a gun to my wife's head. She was acting on some deep need within her, and she was acting alone. She had a lot of pushes along the way, however.

During our last year together, I'd begun to suspect that Norma Jeane was having screen tests done from the hints she dropped in her increasingly infrequent letters that last year when I was at sea. And today, I'm so sorry that she made the decision she did, especially considering the awful way her life ended. Look, I know that sounds so much like sour grapes, and I regret that. But I am sorry. I just can't help but think if she hadn't turned into La MM, she would still be alive today, a happy grandmother surrounded by a new set of babies. Norma Jeane had led a fairly sheltered life, and now, boom! She was suddenly being offered the world, the big time. Money. Fame. Everything she'd ever dreamed of (or claimed she'd dreamed of) as a young girl. And, as it turned out, money and fame translated for her into security and world-wide adulation. It worked. For a short time. I wonder if she loved it all the way she'd thought she would. I wonder if she ever yearned for me when the glitter fell on her. I wonder if she was ever frightened and wished she could curl up warmly and tightly against me, put her sweet head on my chest and sleep safely with me.

And we'd park during those long drives as we discussed the ending in long, long talks, and we'd embrace and we'd tell each other how much we loved one another and it was sublime to be in her arms again and I knew that I loved her still, and so much, and always would. And I knew too that she still loved me. We'd love one another. Always, always.

And another day passed. I tried to tell her things--and I really didn't know much about the movie business, but I'd read about it and because we lived where we did so close to all of that in California, so close to that huge, beckoning, seductive, seducing HOLLYWOOD sign on the mountain. I guess I'd learned a lot about that life by sheer osmosis.

"I think you're deluding yourself, Norma Jeane," I told her as we drove and talked. "This thing you want to get into isn't going to be all peaches and cream. Can you really cope on your own doing this? Without me to help you through it? Shouldn't I be there with you? Norma Jeane," I continued, "You're going to be around people who are wound up tight, people who will push and shove at you, people who'll exploit you. You'll have so- called `friends' around you who won't really be your friends because they'll be jealous of you, like the girls were in your high school, and they'll be full of envy and they'll be after you and I'm afraid they'll get you one day, Norma Jeane. I'm scared that you won't have the strength to withstand them." She reached over and touched my arm, but said nothing. I think that touch was her way of thanking me for my sincere concern, but still, she remained silent.

"And another thing, Norma Jeane," I said. "You'll be under tremendous emotional and physical strain, never having a chance to relax for a second. You'll work so hard all day and will have to go home and stay up all night learning new lines for the next day. Can you do that? Are you strong enough for that?."

"I know, Jimmie," she whispered. "I know all of what you say is true, but I have to do this Jimmie. I have to find out for myself. I just have to do it. Jimmie, dear Jimmie, I just can't not do it, I can't..." And she then became silent and she just stared up at me, and even though her beautiful eyes were now filled with tears I knew from recent past experience that she'd made up her mind, and nothing would change it. Nothing. There was no hope.

CHAPTER 25

And so I did it. I signed the divorce papers, and I drove them over to Norma Jeane's house. My heart was like lead in my chest. And I won't deny that it hurt a little to see her so effervescent that day, happy, practically dancing with high spirits. My God, she could have pretended to be at least a little bit sad, "actress" as she was now.

But then, I was silently glad to realize that this behavior was not entirely because I'd arrived with the papers--well, not completely, that is. She'd just heard that Fox had signed her on as a starlet and would be giving her a new name.

"What'll they be calling you?" I asked as I put the papers on a small table.

"From now on, Jimmie, I'll be called Marilyn Monroe."

"What?" I said. It was such an odd name. It didn't fit my Norma Jeane. No. No. Not at all.

"Marilyn Monroe. Oh, isn't it lovely! Isn't it the most beautiful name you've ever heard?" Norma Jeane just beamed with happiness. She again began to twirl about the room, her arms above her head.

"Oh Jimmie," she gushed, her mouth wide with joy, "please, tell me you like it. It's important to me that you like the name. Please! What do you think of it?"

I could hardly believe she cared what my opinion was about this. But, maybe in fact she did.

"How did they dream that name up?" I asked her, but there was a lump in my throat. Not only was I losing my beloved Norma Jeane, she in fact wouldn't even be Norma Jeane any longer. I was seeing a weird departure here right before my eyes. How could someone right in front of you begin to vanish like that? It was surreal. Horrifying but still mesmerizing in a way. I stood still and watched her. She was "morphing" in front of me. It made me dizzy. Something final was happening, and I knew it. Something dearer to me than anything in the universe was flitting away from me like a small, magical sprite riding off on a sunbeam, never, ever to come back. And I knew it. I knew it. I wanted to reach out and snatch her back, to hold her safely here, in the normal world, with me to protect and love her, but one cannot really catch a sunbeam in one's arms and so I did not try. I had absolutely no more hope.

"I chose Marilyn from one of my grandmothers and Monroe from my mother's maiden name, and the studio liked it! Isn't it just too perfect?" And again, she began a small dance of joy. "It's just so, so beautiful!" And she began to sing the name over and over in her clear, sweet voice as she danced around the room. I watched her through tears and thought I'd never seen such a beautiful sight. And knew I never would again. I never did.

We walked out onto her porch together and I looked down at her. This was awful, terrible. My heart was breaking, but I managed to smile down at her. As hurting as I was, I just could not make myself rain on her parade. I'd always wanted happiness for my darling bride and even now, even with all of this, I just couldn't ruin it for her. I wanted to reach for her, but I smiled instead. If I kept on smiling, my bleeding heart maybe wouldn't show. If I forced my eyes wide, my tears wouldn't spill. But then, I did reach toward her, but pulled back, smiled more widely and I think some tears did spill just a little. Hoping my voice was normal, but hearing a rough growl instead, I said goodbye to my wife and my life, to my Norma Jeane, and I walked off that porch and out of her life.

And suddenly, I was a single man again. I didn't much like it at first, but made the best of it pretty soon and got myself quickly involved with two rather gorgeous young women. One had lovely auburn hair, the other red. Really red. Beautiful!

I'll never forget an incident that happened quite soon after the birth of Marilyn Monroe and at the instant of the death of our marriage.

I was feeling feisty one afternoon and decided to drive by Aunt Ana's where I knew Norma Jeane would be. I had that cute little redhead in the car with me and as I drove past, I honked the horn quite loudly, knowing Norma Jeane would definitely recognize its sound.

It was great! A perfect reaction. Norma Jeane opened the door, looked out at me and the redhead, moved back inside and slammed the door shut. I parked the car, went up to the door and rang the bell.

Norma Jeane jerked the door open. She was livid. She leaned past me and looked in the parked car at the redhead.

"Get in here and close the door," she hissed at me. She grabbed my arm and tried to haul me inside. She was in a complete rage! This was going very well indeed. I made a "wait a second" gesture to my flame-haired date and went inside behind Norma Jeane.

Norma Jeane whirled around and glared at me, her face florid.

"What are you doing with that hussy in our car?" she barked at me.

"Hussy?" I said. "What do you mean hussy? And what do you mean "our" car?"

But now I was beginning to feel real confusion. Why on earth was this former wife of mine throwing such a fit? Did she still have feelings for me? What was the deal? Norma Jeane was just raving mad at me.

"She IS a hussy," she shouted. "That's all she is. Everyone knows that about her. You're not supposed to be going out with girls like that."

"Like what, Norma Jeane? I think she's a very nice young lady. You know, as I recall, you recently divorced me. So I don't see where you get off telling me who I can..."

"Never mind that," she said. "Just don't start going around

with hussies, you hear?"

I drew in a long breath. "Well Norma Jeane," I said quietly, "I guess I'll just have to bring my girlfriends around one at a time for your approval. Will that suit you?"

"That's not funny," she said angrily and pushed me toward the door. I left, not wanting to leave her in such a foul mood, but I just could not help laughing loudly which didn't help the situation at all. I know she heard my laughter. And I know, perverse as it sounds, I enjoyed that she heard it. It was loud laughter, fresh and freeing and genuine. That long laughter coming from my heart and soul began to heal me and it felt wonderful. It was September, 1946.

CHAPTER 26

I was off to the Philippines a few days after the "hussy" incident, and I was glad to go. I was. Losing the love of my life had exhausted me more than I cared to admit. But I refused to sink into self-pity. I would not play the poor-me/poor-victim role, but sometimes, sometimes when I was alone and the memories would come, well, those times were hard. The distraction of sailing off for the Philippines was a blessing.

Naturally, there were no letters from Norma Jeane, although I would hope for them sometimes. But I surely got a lot of news about her. She was really hitting it big and was on a number of magazine covers--now as Marilyn Monroe. I remember one month she graced the covers of six at once. I'd stare at those pictures, trying to see my Norma Jeane, but this young woman's hair was very blonde and her smile was quite different.

But there would be one final visit. We'd made a plan to meet at the dock when I returned. She was to have the car transferred into her name. I'd decided to just give it to her. She'd need it to make all her show-biz appointments and contacts. I'd just get another one.

We met and it was strained, friendly and empty. I drove her back to Aunt Ana's and on the way we stopped for dinner. And it seemed so natural for us to park on the way home from the restaurant, for us to embrace. God it felt so good, so beautiful. My heart began to melt when I was in her arms and it made me feel as if nothing had changed, it made me wish.

"You know, Jimmie," she half whispered, "even though we're divorced now, I still can't help but feel that this--what we're doing now--that this is right somehow."

I pulled back from her and looked into her eyes.

"Norma Jeane, I'm sorry honey, but I just can't agree with you," I said. My emotions were in a terrible conflict, but I knew it was Marilyn who was speaking now, and not the girl I'd married. That remark was a Marilyn Monroe remark, not a Norma Jeane remark.

I wobbled a little just then. I could feel myself wanting to be drawn back, to be with her no matter what. It felt so nice, being with her gave me so much pleasure. I drew in a deep breath.

No. I couldn't. If she happened to make it into the world of film, I'd be married to this famous person and I'd be gone, invisible. She would no longer be Mrs. Jim Dougherty, but I sure as hell would be Mr. Marilyn Monroe and I knew I could not do that. My old-fashionedness kicked in and I remembered that I wanted a home with a wife in it and a bunch of kids. Being married to a woman who had a major career in show business would preclude any of my home-and-hearth plans. I had never heard of any major film queens being married to a sailor. Marilyn Monroe would have soon dumped me anyway, and I'd have been left out in the cold--just as I was now. No. I couldn't do it.

I smiled down at this beautiful, glowing ambitious woman. Who was she? When had she disappeared and re-appeared? I just could not get over it--twins! Maybe that Gemini stuff was true--I'd been married to a lovely wonder-ful woman of dual personalities.

I looked at her and shook my head. Norma Jeane looked sad for a second, then smiled understandingly and I started the engine. I drove her back to Aunt Ana's and I never went back there again--except once, later on when dear old Aunt Ana died. This chapter of my life was positively ended. Norma Jeane Dougherty was gone forever.

CHAPTER 27

But then, I had to speak with Norma Jeane again one more time. I'd gotten her phone number from Grace Goddard because I was getting stung for a lot of traffic tickets--none of which I'd "earned." But I had given the old 1935 Ford coupe to Norma Jeane when we divorced.

"Hey! Norma Jeane!" I said into the phone. "You've got a bunch of tickets out on you. Did you know that?"

"Well Jimmie," she said, "they always just keep hanging those things on the car."

"I imagine they are, dear," trying to sound understanding. "Cops tend to do that when you break the law, but the fact of the matter is, they're going to come and get me for them. Norma Jeane, you promised you'd have the car transferred into your name when I gave it to you. What happened?"

"You? Get you?" she said, ignoring my question. And then Norma Jeane giggled and the sound was lovely to my ears. "Don't be silly. They won't bother you. I'll take care of them," she said.

I told her that would be fine and I hung up, thinking the matter was over. But, I'm not completely dumb. I immediately wrote to the Department of Motor Vehicles, asking them to transfer the car into her name. Norma Jeane had a way of forgetting certain important details and I wasn't about to have my good character sullied by a huge pile of un-responded-to traffic tickets. She was on her own now, for certain!

I still laugh when I recall another time, a couple of years after that when I was at a wrestling match with a bunch of Boy Scouts. I was in the Los Angeles Police Department by then, and worked a lot with kids, and in particular the scouts. The LAPD sponsored this troop and I was the leader.

I was watching the matches when I heard a male voice say "Are you Jim Dougherty?" I thought, "Oh no, another reporter who wants information on Norma Jeane." I sighed.

"Yeah," I said. "I'm Dougherty."

He pushed a pile of papers at me. I looked at them and read that I was being sued by a priest of all things. It seems that before the car had been transferred into Norma Jeane's name, his car had been in a big collision with my old car.

The next day I went to the office of the attorney who was representing the priest.

"I'm no longer the owner of the car," I told the lawyer.

"Oh really?" he said. (This man had a real attitude.) "Well then, Mr. Dougherty," he said, "just exactly who is?"

I gestured to a stack of magazines he had on his windowsill. The top magazine was one called Laff, and there was Norma Jeane in a very sexy pose on top of a surfboard or something like that. It was a beach scene and her body was glorious and provocatively posed. She'd become very famous by then and was on a huge number of magazine covers. I pointed toward the magazine.

"She is," I said. Well, I could almost see dollar signs bursting out of his eyeballs, just like in cartoons. I walked out of his office and never heard another word about the situation.

Of course, that lawyer had no idea at all that there would be no money involved with Marilyn Monroe. She was broke constantly-- broke until the day she died--because she poured every cent she made into advancing her career, into clothes and the newest make-ups, into paying shrinks to keep her sane, and to the people she hired to keep around her. My Norma Jeane never became a wealthy woman from her earnings as an actress.

CHAPTER 28

Yes, there was life for me after Marilyn Monroe. And a good one, too. And one of the good things was a woman named Patricia Scoman.

I'd briefly become somewhat remote from women, but recognized that a lot of emptiness was in my life, now that Norma Jeane was gone. And so when Pat and I began to date, it felt really good. Although, because my mother had sort of set up our introduction, and because I was beginning to have serious feelings for Pat, and because she too worked at Radio Plane, I wondered sometimes if Pat would turn out to have some sort of "secret," too! But that was silly and I knew it. We fell in love.

Pat loved me and my life's interests. She loved children and wanted them, and she was a wonderful cook. She was warm and responsive and great fun to be with, and she eagerly learned how to hunt and fish with me. I was overjoyed when she consented to be my wife.

If Pat had any misgivings about my going into an electrical business, she never said anything. If she'd been doubtful about the man I chose as partner in my new business, she kept silent.

"The war is over," I told her, "and thousands of new homes will be going up. They're all gonna need electricity," I said, and she smiled.

We bought a home in Thousand Oaks, and I began to get a lot of contracting work. And we began having our children--three daughters who I adored then, and continue to love so very dearly.

And then, beloved, kind old Aunt Ana died of a stroke and I went back for the funeral. Pat was reluctant for me to go because she supposed Norma Jeane would be there, and she had developed a rather strong jealousy for my former wife. But I wanted to go because my memories of Aunt Ana were strong. She was a wonderful woman and had been very good to me, and I wanted so much to say goodbye to her. I wept at the funeral parlor. Aunt Ana had been a good woman and my memories of her were strong and happy ones. She'd been everyone's rock, and we all drew from her strength--Norma Jeane included.

And I'm told Norma Jeane actually was at Aunt Ana's home later, but I didn't see her. I think she was in another room in the back, probably with Grace and Doc Goddard. I left and went home. I had no wish to stir up anything within me. I loved Pat now and had my children. Norma Jeane was now relegated to memory only. And I did not touch on her memory too often any more.

I'd begun to develop a sort of "fame," much to my surprise. Several weeks after Aunt Ana died, people began to seek me out, to garner any tidbits they could of information about this new phenomenon, Marilyn Monroe. Pat did not want this, but I love people, regard myself as a "life-loving Irishman," and frankly, I began to enjoy talking to people about my years with Norma Jeane, and I loved telling them how happy and proud I was of her accomplishments. And I genuinely was! She was seen everywhere in photographs-- the beach, amusement parks, out in the country, in parades, the desert, forests. It was just amazing. She was constantly referred to back then as "the budding actress Marilyn Monroe." Imagine--my little Norma Jeane. Yes, it seemed she'd made it after all.

But a cloud was definitely forming. I remember one late afternoon while Pat was preparing dinner, a newspaper photographer walked straight into our yard, unannounced and uninvited. I happened to be out there when he came in and he came over to me, after asking if I was "Jim Dougherty, Marilyn Monroe's former husband." I told him I was.

He asked if he could take some photos of me and after I looked into the kitchen window and not seeing Pat there, I agreed, if he'd hurry to take just a couple and then be on his way. He agreed.

The photographer began circling me taking dozens of pictures from every possible angle. And suddenly, Pat came flying out, with a broom yet, and sent the guy packing. She was furious and I was howling with laughter. Pat did not want me to ever speak of Norma Jeane again. So it was because of Pat's nearly violent feelings on this issue that I made a stupid and unforgettable decision. I destroyed the nearly 200 of Norma Jeane's love letters to me. I'd loved my first wife so much, but I had a new wife now that I loved, the mother of the kids I just worshipped, and so out of respect for her and for them, and to be certain they'd never cause my family any pain or embarrassment, I destroyed those precious, treasured letters.

But still, no matter how much Pat objected, and without any encouragement from me, I was becoming a minor celebrity. Norma Jeane had appeared in two good movies—*The Asphalt Jungle* and *All About Eve* and while the parts were small, they stood out like a diamond lying amongst less glittering gems and she was very, very noticeable. Norma Jeane was now being referred to as "Marilyn," without the Monroe after it--somewhat like Garbo and Harlow and Chaplin had been known. There was only one Marilyn. (Eventually she'd rise to the status of being simply "Monroe." Many of the great ones are called by their last names I guess.)

Even though I was getting a lot of contracting work back then, I discovered that contractors and homeowners frequently do not pay their bills--forcing my own personal bills to remain unpaid. Things were getting tense, and I discovered that my partner might not have been helping things. In time I found myself bankrupt, with my partner having a lot of money, the contents of my store and my truck.

We had to give up the house we loved, and we moved into a trailer park and I was able to land a job pumping gas in a Van Nuys gas station. It was humiliating for me, but I had responsibilities now, children to feed and a wife to care for. I swallowed my pride and did the best job I could.

When old friends from high school came by the station, I

felt the sting of shame. After all, I'd been their Student Body President and here I was pumping gas. But they were OK with it and didn't say anything much, bless them.

Except the ones who were in uniform. Los Angeles Police Department uniforms. Those guys told me I'd be a natural for the department. They told me I should at least fill in the applications and give it a shot, and so eventually, I did, and spent the next 25 years, my happiest years, with the LAPD, and never once did I receive a single complaint from either a citizen, a criminal or another member of the force. Joining the force was one of the very best things I ever did, I honestly know that I contributed to it, and the LAPD enriched my life immeasurably.

But my being a policeman took its toll on Pat, and she disliked being alone so much. To fill her time, she joined a church with which she'd been familiar years ago and now she'd become so involved with it, she was the one who was gone all the time.

I tried to ignore the fact that she was gone for so long, absolutely never home any longer and to concentrate on our three darling daughters, the complete light of my life. I can truly state here that real life for me only began when our babies were born. I had loved kids always and now I had three of my own. They made me just unbelievably happy.

We split, Pat and I, after nearly twenty years. It was 1972 and I found myself a free man again, but it just didn't make me very happy at all. We'd grown apart and had to go our separate ways.

CHAPTER 29

My life went on. As I've stated before, Pat had been intensely jealous of my first wife and so Norma Jeane's name, or Marilyn Monroe's for that matter, was never mentioned in our home. Ever. I really had wanted to go see her movies, but I could not breach that trust, although I do know I'd certainly breached it by meeting with journalists and book authors. I had and still have a lot of guilt around that, but at least I honored my promise to never go to one of La Monroe's movies. (Although once, when Pat was out of the house, I did sneak a look at *Fireball* on TV, with Mickey Rooney. OK, so I'm not perfect!)

But by now, I've seen all of her movies on TV and was surprised to discover what a very good comedienne Norma Jeane had become. And I was stunned at her beauty. I'd always known I'd been married to an absolute knock-out, but in the movies, she was just knock-down, drop-dead gorgeous.

I understand that the movie business is a business of illusion, and that Norma Jeane was in make-up, she'd learned to use her mouth oddly (and very provocatively), she still had that sexy, unique walk, and her voice was trained now, and I'd read rumors of a little plastic surgery which I was doubtful about, but still the realness of Norma Jeane showed through all of that. She had always taken my breath away; in the movies, she very nearly caused me to pass out!

And, she was just so incredibly skilled at her work! Singing! Dancing! Acting! What a talent. She was just gaspingly marvelous. I often sit and watch her still, amazed, astonished at what she'd become.

But it wasn't my Norma Jeane. She'd been lost somewhere along the way. Maybe she'd been absorbed by this Marilyn Monroe person, the sexy movie goddess. My Norma Jeane was gone forever from me, long before she'd become lost forever to the world. World one, Jim Dougherty zero. But that's OK. I guess she was destined to belong to the world. But I sure got to keep her for a little while, and it was good, it indeed was good.

Did Norma Jeane want to become a sex symbol? I have to think no. I think ultimately she wanted to be recognized as a great actress and from all I've read, she went after that, hard--but she grabbed at the sex-symbol thing as a chance to make it in show business, as maybe a step toward being a noted actress. She bought into it and promoted it vigorously. Was it the wrong move? I don't think so. A great many actresses back then started out as song and dance ladies, maybe comediennes, and moved sometimes easily (sometimes not) into serious acting, so if Norma Jeane was desirous of becoming a serious dramatic actress, then she probably grabbed at the sex symbol thing as a boost to that goal. It was a crapshoot. It may have worked eventually, but sadly for her, it never happened in her lifetime. But I think she was on the edge of being taken seriously. She was trying so hard. Her last film, *The Misfits*, showed that side of her I think.

And yet there's no doubt she enjoyed that sexy image. Adulation from the world and even from the few mattered a very great deal to her. Abandoned so often as a kid, she grasped at all the love and so-called security she could get. But, Norma Jeane/Marilyn Monroe died before she had a chance to ripen and mature into a serious actress. She was getting there, working toward it, toward maybe being a great character actress if not a principal. Remember Bette Davis and Susan Hayward? They too worked at their craft and I really do not think that their first concerns were being sexy--it was the work they focused on. The same with Norma Jeane. But it never really happened for her. She was frightened that she'd be a freak, a sexy non-human with a fabulous body; a joke. What a fight she had on her hands! It was a fight she lost.

CHAPTER 30

I'd like to speak here about my take on the ethics of journalism. I've been asked so often about my short time with this now very famous woman. And of course, she's even more famous today than she was when she was alive.

I've always spoken the absolute truth about my time with her. I've been interviewed so many times I really can't count them at this point. Television shows from all over the world have asked for an interview.

I wrote my own book called "The Secret Happiness of Marilyn Monroe," hoping that people would finally know the truth about her early life with me. I'm hoping now that this new book will explain even more fully how this woman really was, that people will know of her truthfully, know that she was just a person, but a good person, simple and complex both, innocent and yearning for love.

But it seems that people don't believe. I've been accused of coloring the truth, embellishing it. Norma Jeane's life was so unusual, so exciting and unique that there's never been any need to embellish a single thing when I'm interviewed. But still the people who write of her after I've told them about her, twist all my words, invent things that never happened.

For example, the rape story which I've previous mentioned, which she supposedly endured at the hands of her foster-father. Now my understanding of rape is forced penile penetration of a female's vagina. This just could not have happened. On our wedding night, there was a 100% indication to me that she was definitely a virgin.

But of course, that doesn't make great copy the way a rape story does, and in her eagerness for fame, Norma Jeane didn't deny any of these tales when they cropped up like mushrooms after a summer rain and if in fact she did not invent them, then she surely encouraged them. By herself? Or because the studios told her to. I'll never know. I often wonder if she'd lived if she'd have regretted allowing all of those awful rumors to be born, to stay alive and to grow like hideous cancers. I wonder if she'd ever write about them and deny them. But of course, now no one will ever know.

Norma Jeane made it, she became a huge star, she was on her way to becoming a really respected actress. She met the very famous and the not so famous. She went everywhere. I was so proud of her. Why do writers have to exaggerate about her? The truth is fascinating enough, isn't it?

I kept on hearing about her. Everyone did, but because I'd been married to her, I heard a lot more.

Frankly, I never have believed all those Kennedy rumors about their being involved in Norma Jeane's death. And of course, the individual who claims to have been married to her after our marriage, I consider absolutely bogus. I won't even mention his name here. He was never married to her, but has managed to cleverly "prove" that he was and to perpetuate this story. How odd it is that the engraved old watches "To XXX with all my love Marilyn" show engraving that is very fresh and new looking. How convenient that all the supposed records of that Mexican marriage have managed to have "been destroyed." Right. Well, there are some people who will always be willing to feed themselves from the dead body of someone else. You know, the way Buzzards feed from corpses.

There was one strong incident I'll never forget, which fits in with all that I'm trying to say here in this chapter. In 1952, my sister Billie gave a story to a magazine written by her about Norma Jeane's home life with the Doughertys.

I was at work at the LAPD and suddenly, completely unexpectedly, Norma Jeane called me. She was angry about the article and kept insisting that the article "was just not fair."

I had not read it and I told her that. "But," I said, "if it's your perception that it was not a fair article, then of course, it probably was not."

And then she demanded "how could you allow this to happen?" Allow? I didn't live with my sister and had no control over what she did. As a matter of fact, I hadn't seen Billie for a very long time and hadn't been in touch. Norma Jeane was angry. I was becoming angry, too. After all, I was at work with dozens of people around me and I had to endure being scolded by her for something I had no responsibility for.

"Look, Norma Jeane," I said. "I have not read the article. I don't even know where it appeared and I haven't been in touch with my sister for a long time. Furthermore, I do not think she would ever deliberately write anything to hurt you."

"But Jimmie," she said, "nothing in that article was even true."

"Well, I'm sorry about that, Norma Jeane. Billie may have taken some facts and made up a story around them. And let's not forget that maybe she gave the facts as she saw them and someone else added the stuff you're so upset about. It happens. Stories about actresses are always twisted and exaggerated. You of all people should know about that Norma Jeane, being in the business you're in."

I was perplexed. I just didn't understand the call and had no idea what she wanted me to do about the article. After all, it was written and published. Too late to do anything about it now. She should have known that the written word was always twisted when it came to the famous.

And then, to make it worse, she said, her voice very sharp, "Well, it seems to me as if someone's just trying to make money." (Today someone might respond to that by saying "well, duh. Yeah. That's how it works, honey.") But I didn't say anything like that. And frankly, I couldn't really even answer that statement, so I just said "well, thanks for telling me about it, Norma Jeane" and again assured her that the Dougherty family had not been in collusion with that story by Billie. And anyway, Norma Jeane was so enormously popular by that time she probably had begun to believe her own press.

I imagine my sister Billie's article (and nearly all of it was about my marriage to Norma Jeane) was a small fantasy, an exaggeration of how things really were and then words and words and words were added to by the magazine people. After publication, Billie spent the money she got (probably not a great deal) and forgot all about it. I think the media and the magazine exaggerated the article, and that was what was embarrassing and hurtful to Norma Jeane.

Our phone call was winding down, and getting nowhere. I had to speak up.

"You know, Norma Jeane," I said. "I'm upset about this too, now that you've told me about it, and I'm sorry it happened, and sorry it has caused you discomfort. But I want you to know something. Pat and I have three wonderful baby daughters, and they know nothing about that part of my life, with you. They are being brought up in complete ignorance of it."

There was a long pause, complete silence. And then, her voice soft and sad, my former wife quietly said, "I understand." And she hung up.

I do not know if I made my point, but the call had caught me so completely by surprise that I did not have time to organize my thoughts. She called me in anger but ended up more injured, I think, by the phone call than by that stupid article. I felt then and still feel very, very bad about that. But I can in all honesty say that I reacted in the best way I could and I told her the absolute truth. I won't soon forget her sadly soft "I understand" statement. I think she was telling me she knew I'd finally found happiness with another woman and had the children I'd wanted so dearly. This truly was the final parting.

The leeches, the so called "journalists" and the show-biz types who dogged her so were, in my opinion, greatly responsible for her deterioration--and therefore they were ultimately responsible for her death. I mean by that that she was so preoccupied with trying to keep herself sane and focused and balanced, that she'd forget things. But they dogged her horribly. She couldn't even have a nice, respectable private nervous breakdown without them cornering her and forcing her to face them when she was at her lowest. Oh God that film of her being led through that crowd of vampires by a grinning nurse, pulling the collar of her coat up over her face and turning her poor, tortured face to the wall so they couldn't see or photograph her. I know a lot of Norma Jeane's public "grievings" were staged. I think that time in perfect make-up and hair when she stood gently sobbing in front of a crowd of news people after her nine month marriage to DiMaggio was over was total PR and hype and beautifully planned, but not that short film of her at her very lowest, her nervous breakdown, turning to the wall that way---oh it hurts me to see that and still, all these decades later, they have to show that poor woman's torment. I do not have an awful lot of kind things to say about the vultures who pursue the famous that way and rob them of their most private and intimate moments.

But, back to the issue of her too-early death; Norma Jeane forgot lots of things when we were married, but as she got more and more into this awful and wonderful dream of hers, she just couldn't keep anything straight, and so I can't help but feel that she took so many pills to get herself to wake up (she was so notoriously late for everything because she had terrible insomnia) that at the end of the day, she had to take a bunch more to get herself to sleep at night. I think she just forgot and overdosed. And I blame the world for that, to a point. If only the news hounds and movie moguls had just let her be. But no. They just kept on pounding and pounding at her. They pushed and pushed, exaggerated about her and hounded her constantly like drooling mad dogs, their fangs out for her all the time. She couldn't hold that mob back much longer. She got so tired. Everyone wanted a piece of her, and she just finally ran out of pieces. I wish I could have saved her. I wish I could have put the pieces of Norma Jeane Dougherty back together.

CHAPTER 31

One of the very best things I ever did was to join the Los Angeles Police Department. Because of my contribution there, I can state with absolute certainty that my life has mattered. I made a difference. I changed lives. I contributed to the betterment of some young people which was the most important of my accomplishments. It was good.

I advanced fairly rapidly. I began as all rookies do as a policeman on a beat. I then became an instructor and enrolled at the University of California where I earned a teaching credential. I continued to take courses and because of my youthful knowledge of guns and shooting with dead accuracy, my reputation as a crack shot grew, and I was eventually assigned to travel around Los Angeles (and especially in public schools) doing PR work for the police department by giving demonstrations of my shooting prowess.

One of the best acts I worked up was when I'd ask a woman in the audience if I might borrow her diamond ring for a few moments. She'd usually agree and I'd lean a playing card up against a safe, thick target with the edge facing me. I'd then look into one of the facets of the diamond, see the reflection of that card, take aim and shoot, and split that card with the bullet. Hard to believe, but I was that good. Sorry to sound immodest, but the truth is the truth!

And I still might still be as good a shot, even well into my seventies. OK, I still am! Let's call a spade a spade, after all. Today I live on a fabulously beautiful lake in Maine and own a boat. I heard recently that someone talked about the possibility of my boat being stolen, and my neighbor responded, "Yeah, anyone who'd steal that boat would get 300 yards away, Dougherty would take aim and the guy's head would be gone.")

In time during my tenure at the LAPD, because of my

shooting ability, the Deputy Chief of Police ordered me to collect thirty riflemen from the force and to qualify them in a variety of weapons. And this was the fledgling S.W.A.T. training which (still) stands for Special Weapons and Tactics team. This was top secret stuff and not known to the world until 1974 when knowledge of this group's enormous capabilities burst into public awareness when they were called in to lead the attack on the Symbionese Liberation Army--the kidnappers of the famous Patty Hearst who'd ended up embracing that insane group, going against all that she'd been born to and embarking on a sweeping crime spree with them. I guess she was brainwashed by those crazies, but still I think she might have been somewhat stronger. But I wasn't there and don't know but still I don't have much respect for that sort of behavior.

Did I get advancements in the department because of my marriage to Norma Jeane? Hardly. As I look back now on both of our lives, I see that we both advanced in professions we loved at about the same pace. I'd come through World War II, had remarried and had my three darling daughters. Marilyn--well, everyone on this earth knows what she did with her life.

I will always wonder if she occasionally wished she had a stable family life, and children. From all I've read about her marriages and her life and supposed multiple abortions (how can that be? She so desperately wanted children. Did men force her to do that? That hurts me to think about---) it appeared that she yearned constantly for the wonderful things of life that I'd been blessed with. Maybe it turned out that I really did have the best of our two lives. I was never lonely and scared, as I know she was. I felt fulfilled, with my job, my wife, my beloved children. Did she? I think not. I pray she did. I think she did not.

CHAPTER 32

I've already explained why I destroyed the 200 love letters I'd gotten from Norma Jeane during my time in the Merchant Marine during World War II. I did that out of respect for my wife, Pat, who just could not stand to think of my being married to what had turned out to be this famously sexy woman who'd done a nude calendar and whose face was being seen everywhere every day. And, as I've mentioned, because I loved Pat and didn't wish to cause her any unhappiness, I never even mentioned Norma Jeane's (or Marilyn Monroe's) name in my own household.

But I have to admit that there were---well, occasional times when I sort of dreamed about Norma Jeane's and my paths crossing. After all, we both lived in the Los Angeles area. It could happen!

In 1950, I was assigned to crowd control in front of Grauman's Chinese Theatre where they were holding a big premier of *The Asphalt Jungle*, in which Norma Jeane was appearing, and I have to say she was pretty good in it.

The limousines began to appear and it was my job to make sure they got through the crush of fans. And I'll be honest and state that each time a blonde emerged from a limo, my heart would jump. Oh, I so wanted to see her, to speak with her again, to be sure she was all right and healthy, that she was taking care of herself and mostly that she was happy. It would have soothed my soul somewhat, to see her and hear her and maybe feel her touch for an instant. Would I have been able to determine all of that even if I'd only gotten a quick glance of her that night? Yes. I knew her so very well that all I had to do was take a quick look into her eyes, to hear a word or two from her lips. I'd have known. Yes, I would have known.

But she never showed up. Had she been sick that night?

Was she too frightened to face that crowd? Of perhaps seeing me? After all, she knew I was in the LAPD. I so wanted to get close to her, to see if she was all right. I went home that night feeling disappointment, stung because I didn't get to see my Norma Jeane. And even though it's my habit and my lifelong MO to dust myself off when disappointment hits, sometimes it's hard to do that. I can always do it, but some of those times are harder than others and I really was extremely disappointed that I didn't see her. I had no one to talk with about it. Certainly not Pat. And so I went home and acted as if nothing had happened.

Is it true that we never really stop loving someone with whom we've been in love in another part of our lives? Is it true that a tiny, secret piece of our hearts always belong to that person for the remainder of our lives? Yes. I think so. I have never stopped loving Norma Jeane Dougherty. I don't expect I ever will. I don't plan to and to be completely honest, I do not want to.

It had been gnawing at me for a long time, at my mind, at my innards. A bad feeling.

Something was wrong. Something bad was about to happen. And it all had to do with Norma Jeane. Whether or not she was aware of it, there was still a strong bond between us and I could feel things about her--I knew, I felt things. I was worried, helpless. Something bad was out there. Something dark. Something terrible, and I knew it was connected somehow to Norma Jeane. But, like the onset of an earthquake I was unable to do a thing to stop it. I was powerless. I'd been away from Norma Jeane for so long that by the time 1962 rolled around, there was nothing on this green earth I could do about my uneasiness, my forebodings. They just were there, scratching quietly at me, known.

A couple of years before this, I'd been having a few drinks with some friends at a New Year's Eve party and suddenly, they dared me to call Norma Jeane. Yes, I'd kept her phone number in a tiny black book I carried with me since our last conversation when she called in such a state of anger over the article my sister Billie wrote about her.

I called. My hands shook and I hoped no one would notice. But a stranger answered, some person I did not know who'd been assigned that old phone number, and again it was driven home to me that the beautiful, naive young woman I'd married who'd become so famous would hardly have a known phone number. My disappointment and sadness was keen that night, but again, I hoped it didn't show. Because I'm a ham and frankly a born actor, I acted that night, but my heart hurt a little. Norma Jeane didn't live there any more.

And I don't know. Maybe it was that night when I finally, totally accepted the fact that my Norma Jeane had become Marilyn Monroe.

In the past few years, I'd been unable to resist reading the gossip columns carefully, and gradually, I noticed there was hardly any mention of her any more. Marilyn's marriages to Joe DiMaggio and Arthur Miller had been tragically sad, troubled, awful for her. Perhaps for all of them. She'd been divorced, childless and cast adrift. The papers revealed multiple abortions, which I just would not believe. I knew she was alone now. I did not know that her horrible ordeal, her final one, was about to happen to her, and I would not be with her to help her. Oh God, to save her.

In June of 1962, I read she'd been fired by her studio. Marilyn Monroe! A legend in her own time. Fired. That was odd. It was also strange and shocking. I knew she'd been difficult to work with, endlessly late to her movie sets costing the studios thousands and then millions of dollars. She was undependable, so filled with those old dark moods which were coming more often, her terrors. And then those drugs to make her sleep made it so she could not focus while awake. Even legends can get to be a liability, an annoyance and nuisance. Even legends can be replaced in Hollywood. In that town, there's always a new legend waiting in the wings.

CHAPTER 33

It was still dark that dawn when the phone rang. I sat up in bed, Pat next to me. I picked up the phone and heard my friend Sgt. Jack Clemmons tell me she was dead. Oh God. Norma Jeane, my darling.

Suicide? No. She would have written a note to say good-bye. She had been on the phone. They found the phone in her small hand. Did someone know she was in trouble? Robert Kennedy? Peter Lawford? Someone else? And were they so terrified about losing their careers, their reputations that they did nothing? If this is true, then they are accountable.

But in the end, what else was there? Norma Jeane died by her own hand, accidentally, by herself and because of herself. I refuse to believe otherwise.

First marriages frequently have a profound effect on a person. I know mine surely did. I think every single day about the too short time Norma Jeane and I had together. Our four married years together were like an island of love and security for her, for both of us. But for Norma Jeane, it had become a sense of identity for her and today because of her, one of my identities is the fact that she was my wife. Not my only one, but it's definitely there. Married to me, Norma Jeane had finally become "someone." She'd been just sort of "there" till then, something to be dealt with, a bother, and, a kind of see-through child. A problem and annoyance to be dealt with.

Today, it would be called "sexist" if I were to suggest that Norma Jeane Mortenson (Baker) Dougherty felt as if she'd finally become a real person when she married me and took my name. But in fact, that's what happened to her and we both knew it. She finally allowed herself to think that as my wife, she'd never be abandoned again. She felt safe with me. Protected. She showed me and told me that very thing. Repeatedly. I know Norma Jeane held tightly to being Norma Jeane Dougherty somewhere in her heart, and that she never let it go, or let me go. She never "officially" became Marilyn Monroe. She had not ever registered her name change. How do I know this? Because when Marilyn Monroe went to Korea to entertain the troops after her marriage to Joe Dimaggio, I saw a photograph of the permit she had to use to get onto the base. A pass, I guess. It did not say Marilyn Dimaggio. It said Norma Jeane Dimaggio. she had remained Norma Jeane Dougherty all that time, and I will never forget how sore of heart that made me feel.

What haunts me is my wondering if those old, frantic feelings came back to her in the years she lived after our divorce. If what I read is true, then they did and it hurts my very soul to think those old terrors came back to live with her again and I could never be there to soothe and reassure her and make her feel sheltered. The idea of that torments me.

When she became Marilyn Monroe, she put our years together behind her. That's as it should be when people divorce. They must move through the pain and move on. I did. I know she did too. I'd read that she would occasionally refer to me as a "good" person, using that old familiar word she liked to use when she talked about me to others so very long ago. And I cannot deny that it hurt when I would read that she would say that ours was a marriage of convenience.

But on one level, I guess it was. It kept her from going to an orphanage. So yes, looking at it that way, it certainly was a "marriage of convenience." But oh, how lucky we were to have fallen so deeply in love when we married each other. Deeply like an ocean is deep. Bottomlessly. I am still stunned at the depth and enormity of our passion for each other.

And now I have to say Bravo, Norma Jeane! You did it! You did what you set out to do. You desperately wanted endless love, and now, that's what you have. They tell me fresh flowers are placed near your crypt constantly, and oh my God how it pains my heart to say the words "your crypt." You finally won the thing you were on such a fervent quest for, Norma Jeane, my darling, wistful wife, the thing you so desperately craved; to be loved unendingly by the world. You are more famous and more loved today than you were in life, and in life you were loved more than you knew! You've achieved what your poor, dear heart wished for--unending adulation. Everyone knows and cares about you now, Norma Jeane, even people who were born long after you died.

If there is life after death, and I believe there is, there is so much I want to ask Norma Jeane/Marilyn Monroe. She left me with so many questions I never got the answers to. I was there at the very end of Norma Jeane and the very beginning of Marilyn Monroe. I never got a chance to say goodbye to either woman. I wish I had.

But you know I never wanted to say goodbye to you, Norma Jeane. You know I had to go into the service. I had no choice in the matter. Everyone had to go. Remember I picked a branch of the service that would allow me to come home more often than members of the Army or Navy or Airforce or Marines. A branch of the service that would keep me out of as much danger as those guys were in. I did it so I'd have a better chance of coming home to you because I knew you needed me desperately and I had promised you that I'd always be there for you. The Merchant Marines was the best choice for both of us, but with all of that planning, that branch of the service kept me away from you long enough for you to be lured away from me. It killed me piece by piece to have to leave you all those times, but of course each time it got easier. For you. And for all of us who had to leave those we loved, the good-byes were the hardest part.

Had you been lonely? Sad while I was gone? Had you

begun to feel abandoned yet again? Fearful I'd die some-where far away and never come back to you? In the way back of your heart, did you think you'd better hurry to find some way to discover everlasting love for yourself in case mine would be taken from you? Sometimes when I think about you and our time, I wonder if it was in your, maybe, unconscious hope to get thousands, no, millions of people to love you so that in case some of them stopped, others would be in position to take their place.

Oh sweetheart, why didn't you tell me about your secret dreams? We used to be able to talk about everything. We could have worked something out, I know. I wish I'd known. I wish you'd trusted me enough to tell me. You trusted Aunt Ana. She knew. Why couldn't I know?

I've never been able to forget you, Norma Jeane. I see your face every single day of my life; in the post office, in books at the library and bookstores, on TV, posters, T-shirts, life-size cut-outs in stores, on mugs. It is amazing, Norma Jeane. You should see all of this! You did it, my darling. You did it. I'm proud of you, sweetheart. So proud!

On our final day together, I remember not having the chance to say all the words I wanted to or should have said to you, my darling Norma Jeane. I was hurting. I was angry, and frightened at the thought of spending the rest of my life without you. I was afraid of being lonely without you.

I know I'll see you again. Maybe soon. When that time comes, I'll be able to ask you all these things I've wondered about all these years. For instance I'd ask you if you really loved me back then, and please, you'll forgive me for sounding whiny. But you know it is a question that rises up in my mind from time to time, because to my way of think-ing, however old fashioned, if someone truly loves another person, they pretty much stay that way or work on any problems so that the love can remain undamaged. Did you truly love me? You said you did. You acted as if you did. You showed me over and over. How modest you were; you loved to be nude in our home, in front of me. But if anyone were to see you that way, you'd have been mortified. You had such a sense of pride, spirituality, chastity. How could they ever have talked you into being naked for the world to see? Who did that to you? By doing that, had they finally pulled away all of what was left of Norma Jeane from you?

I really didn't ask you the things I wanted to that day, Norma Jeane. I can't really remember what we said too clearly, except that we stood there at the end of our time together, at the end of you and the birth of Marilyn Monroe.

I know I'll see you again, my beloved Norma Jeane. I miss you so dearly. You were my heart's darling. I love you.

THE END

EPILOGUE

On March 23 in 1974, I officially retired from the Los Angeles Police Department, closing a rich, multi-textured chapter in my life, a chapter filled with varied and fabulous experiences, many dangerous, many thrilling, and all important. These were years of great personal growth and an accumulation of lifetime friendships. The cops I worked with were the finest. I was very fortunate.

I was only 52 when I retired, and divorced from Pat, but I'd put in 25 good years and wanted to do other things. Spending time hunting and fishing was one of them. Perhaps I'd get involved in local politics. I'd earned a decent pension from my years on the LAPD, and felt comfortable about leaving and beginning a new chapter in my life.

The LAPD gave me a huge party which they advertised for a week on the radio and in newspapers. Even my ex-wife Pat attended which meant a lot to me. After all, she'd been the one who'd lived through all the long nights while I was on duty. And, she'd presented me with the three most precious people in my life.

Executives from Jack Webb productions came too, remembering the work we'd done with them to help make that famous old show (The Jack Webb Show) accurate and successful. Everyone I'd ever worked with attended. They even had to sell tickets!

On the final night the LAPD presented me with an enormous framed testimonial, hand painted and gold-leafed. It told of my accomplishments, including a long list of praise. And because they loved me, the men and women of the LAPD shouted the rousing cheer I can still hear:

Hooray for Jim!

Hooray at last!

Hooray for Jim!

He's a horse's ass!

Norma Jeane would have loved being there. I can hear her laughing now.

And then Rita, my lovely, my wonderful Rita. She was beautiful, sexy. A small blonde with a figure that just knocked your eyes out! (And she's got it still.) I could see she loved me immediately. Today she is still a dazzling woman no one believes is, like me, well into her seventies. My ravishing, wonderful Rita had also been married before and had suffered because of that union, perhaps worried for a while that if she took a chance and remarried she might again suffer the awful abuse she endured at the hands of her first husband. But never once did she have a moment's fear from me. I respect women too much to do that to them. And I respect and love this woman devotedly. Like me, Rita also had daughters.

And so Rita made me the happiest man alive when she told me she'd marry me. We moved from California to Arizona together and eventually to Maine. She'd been born in that beautiful state, and we continue to live there today and it's where we went to end our days. We live in a tiny town on a huge lake and I fish and hunt to my heart's content, and it is beautiful and it is Paradise.

My Rita is an extremely talented artist. Her astonishing paintings hang all over our home and elicit so many compliments. But she won't sell them because she says they are a part of her. I understand her feelings on this matter, but it is a shame these beautiful artworks aren't seen by more people.

Rita makes my life complete. She laughs at my jokes, even when I've told them (and she's heard them) dozens of times. She's listened to my telling and retelling of the Marilyn Monroe stories and all the stories of my youth and she could probably recite them right along with me. But still, she sits in rapt attention, making me feel special. She's made huge lunches for the countless TV crews who've come to our home to spend nearly the whole day so they could interview me. She sits quietly in the background, and again, listens to the same old stories.

Rita fusses over me, makes me take my medicine, makes me lose weight. She is a wonderful, inventive cook, too. Smart and funny and intense, she is very good to me.

When I look at Rita, and I do that a lot, I sometimes wonder how I could ever have gotten so lucky. She has many gifts, but one of her greatest is a complete absence of jealousy. I am allowed to speak about my first or second marriages any time I wish, and she listens and is never jealous.

And anyway, Rita is fascinated about the Norma Jeane time in my life and amazingly never tires of hearing those stories and encourages me to pursue any requests for appearances on radio or TV, and to speak to anyone who wishes to interview me anywhere in the world. She encourages me to fly all over the world for these interviews too, and so I go. And the requests still come in constantly. Frequently from children who are doing a class project or writing papers. I always smile when they call. How do they know about Marilyn Monroe? Well, they seem to, although I often wonder if perhaps their teachers have "put them up to it" because they themselves still love my Norma Jeane and want to know about her. I am always happy to share my memories of her, and especially to kids. It's important to me to keep her memory truthful and alive.

Amazingly, Rita is actually very defensive about Norma Jeane and if she ever hears anyone say an unkind or unflattering word about her, or an untruth, I suggest they duck! She respects Norma Jeane's memory and considers that the past is just that--the past. It is now that matters most to my Rita. She and I are a couple now and today is what matters to her. Rita and Norma Jeane would have been good friends.

And now in my late seventies, I've got some old age aches and pains, but I'm still active. I hunt and fish in season. I get out on our boat whenever I can, and still work around our home. I don't want to ever leave Maine and I even think that in the dead of winter, too.

And I'm still frequently flown to places all around the country and Canada (and once to Japan) to appear on television because of my first wife, or TV (or radio) people from famous talk shows come to my home to interview me. I dabble in local politics when asked and I'm frequently asked by the local law enforcement people to share my knowledge from when I was on the LAPD. I've been able to implement a great deal of my police experience here in Maine, especially with problems involving kids. I love kids and I always see good in all of them, even the worst of the lot.

Rita and I live in a wonderful home on a huge lake in this most beautiful state of Maine, and we share a great dog, a Yorky, named Mikkie-NickieTu. We're close to all our children and see them frequently.

I have never been so happy. I've had a blessed life.

- **To Norma Jeane With Love, Jimmie** -Jim Dougherty as told to LC Van Savage (2001) ISBN 1-888725-51-6 The sensitive and touching story of Jim Dougherty's teenage bride who later became Marilyn Monroe. Dozens of photographs. "The Marilyn Monroe book of the year!" As seen on TV. 5½X8¼, 216 pp, $16.95 **MacroPrintBooks**™ edition ISBN 1-888725-52-4, 8¼X6½, 16 pt, 290pp, $24.

- **Virginia Mayo—The Best Years of My Life** (2002) Autobiography of film star Virginia Mayo as told to LC Van Savage. From her early days in Vaudeville and the Muny in St Louis to the dozens of hit motion pictures, with dozens of photographs. ISBN 1-888725-53-2, 5½ X 8¼, 300 pp, $16.95

BeachHouse
Books

BeachHouseBooks
PO Box 7151
Chesterfield, MO 63006-7151
(636) 394-4950
www.beachhousebooks.com

Item	Each	Quantity	Amount
Missouri (only) sales tax 6.925%			
Shipping per order)			$5.00
	Total		
Ship to Name:			
Address:			
City State Zip:			

Made in the USA
San Bernardino, CA
14 February 2013